The
SOLUTION
to SOCIAL ANXIETY

**Break Free From the Shyness
That Holds You Back**

DR. AZIZ GAZIPURA

DISCLAIMER

The information in this book reflects the opinions of the author and is not intended to replace medical or psychological advice, or any other professional advice. This book is not intended to diagnose or treat any psychological or medical conditions or disorders. If you are in need of psychological or medical treatment, consult with a certified and licensed professional before determining whether the information in this book should be used.

Printed in the United States of America

First Printing, 2013

ISBN 978-0-9889798-0-2

LCCN 2013913552

Aziz Gazipura, Psy.D.
1210 S.E. Oak Street, Suite 1
Portland, Oregon, USA

socialconfidencecenter.com

To Tony, Candace, and Elliot
Thank you for teaching me how to set myself free.

Also By Dr. Aziz

E-Books

Five Steps To Unleash Your Inner Confidence
How To Overcome Your Fear Of Public Speaking

Video Training Programs

Confidence Unleashed
30 Days To Dating Mastery

Contents

INTRODUCTION

I am glad you have come across this book. If you are suffering or struggling in your life right now, I understand. I spent many years stuck in a place of debilitating shyness that prevented me from speaking up, meeting people, going on dates, and having satisfying relationships. I know the pain of this shyness in a very deep and intimate way.

The worst part about this shyness was not that I couldn't go after what I wanted in my life. It wasn't that I felt nervous and tense in my body much of the time. It wasn't even that I was unable to bring myself to ask women out or date because of my intense fear of rejection. All of these aspects of my shyness were very painful and I struggled with each of them, but the worst part about it was that *I believed I was going to be stuck like this forever.*

I saw other guys, including friends of mine, who were somehow able to do what I could not. They would make jokes, speak up in groups, and flirt with women. I saw myself as somehow different, or less than they were. This gap between them and me seemed like an insurmountable chasm, leaving me on the outskirts forever.

If you relate to these struggles, and you fear that things might not change, I am especially glad you found this book. It is essentially written to a version of myself from 15 years ago. In it I am sharing everything I have learned about how to break free from the confines of fear and anxiety that held me back.

I have applied everything you will read in this book either on myself or with one of the hundreds of men I have worked with over the last decade. It is my sincerest hope that these ideas, exercises, tools, and tips help you realize something that shifted my life forever—that you are not stuck this way, that it is entirely possible to find a well of courage inside of your heart that will drive you to overcome the challenges you are facing. It will drive you to face your fears, rejection, and failure in order to create the friendships, career, relationships, and life you truly want. As you do this, you will see just how much of your social anxiety was based on old, inaccurate stories and ideas about yourself. You will start to see the truth about yourself—who you are, and what you have to offer the world—and life will start to look a lot brighter.

I wish you good luck on this journey, and I am excited to be with you along the way.

Dr. Aziz
Portland, OR
2013

AUTHOR'S NOTE:

Throughout this book you will find real examples of shy and socially anxious men and women who struggle with the exact same challenges you do. Sometimes when we are anxious we can look around at others and assume that they do not have any of these problems. We can think that no one else gets as afraid and conclude that there must be something terribly wrong with us.

This could not be further from the truth. Actually, social anxiety affects over 15 million Americans, and over 50% of people identify as shy.

These challenges are incredibly common and you are not alone.

You are not broken or defective. In fact, there is nothing wrong with you. You are simply experiencing an uncomfortable and challenging pattern that is limiting your choices and options.

In the book you will find *Shy Quotes*—these are things that shy clients have shared about their experiences in sessions with me. They can highlight some of your own shy patterns and provide a sense of relief that you are in fact not alone in your shyness. Millions of other people experience these same challenges every day.

Names, details, and other identifying information about clients I have worked with have been changed substantially, while maintaining the essence of their struggle or challenge. To that end, any resemblance to an actual person is entirely coincidental.

A NOTE ON GENDER AND SEXUAL ORIENTATION:

The majority of clients I work with are men who are seeking to enhance their confidence, often in the area of dating and creating relationships with women. As such, the majority of the examples and case studies refer to these men.

However, the material in this book is applicable and absolutely effective if you are a woman or a gay man seeking to develop relationships with other men. For the sake of simplicity, throughout this book I primarily refer to the reader as "he" and a potential dating partner as "she." Please alter the pronouns to fit your specific situation, as I believe the underlying psychology of social anxiety and confidence is the same, whether you are man or woman, heterosexual or homosexual.

PART 1—THE PROBLEM

One

STUCK IN SHYNESS

If you are reading this book, then you know what shyness is. And you know what "social anxiety" is, even if you have never used that term.

You know that tight feeling in your throat and the thumping in your chest before it is your turn to speak in a group. You know that intense feeling of fear and dread before you are going to start a conversation with that attractive person. And you know that nagging worry in your mind that just will not stop: What do they think of me? Did I do that right? Could they tell I was nervous?

How about that tense feeling in your stomach when you are about to meet someone new? When you are in that horribly awkward moment after you have both exchanged names and are standing there looking at each other, waiting, *hoping* that you will be able to think of something to say. You frantically scramble for some question, some observation, something, *anything* to say, but all your mind gives you is: *Oh my god, you don't have anything to say. What's wrong with you? Say something!*

The silence in this moment is not the sweet, peaceful silence you experience when you wake up before dawn, or go for a hike in the forest alone. No, this silence is painful, pregnant with expectation and loaded with pressure. It feels like your skin is crawling, and you begin hoping one of the chandeliers will fall from the ceiling so you can make an unnoticed and hasty escape.

Can you relate? When was the last time you experienced something like this? If you are anxious around people, then you might have this experience all too often. In fact, this might be your primary experience of meeting people. You might have experienced this so often that you say things like:

I don't like going to parties.
I hate meeting new people.
I hate small talk.
People there are so boring and only talk about stupid things that don't matter.
I'm so awkward.
I don't have anything interesting to say.
No one would want to talk with me when they could be talking to someone better.
I can't do that, I have social anxiety.
There's something wrong with me.

What else do you say to yourself about your social life and social abilities? How do you feel about socializing, about being around others? Do you feel anxious, tense, stuck, frustrated, discouraged, or hopeless? Do you feel like you've tried everything and nothing works?

And yet you are reading this book. Perhaps there is a sliver of hope left. Perhaps you have not tried everything. What if it were possible for you to shift something inside of yourself, so that you could have better conversations with people you just met? Better yet, what if you could actually enjoy those conversations? What if you shifted something in yourself so you did not feel that nervous about meeting someone new? What if you were not really worried about whether they were going to like you? How would you behave? What would you say or do?

The truth is, it is entirely possible to shift from social anxiety to social confidence. It is possible to feel relaxed and curious when meeting new people, to feel nervous yet excited before flirting with someone, and to feel elated after making friends or going on a date. The anxiety and fear you feel around others is the result of a learned pattern. It is a pattern of specific thoughts, feelings, and behaviors—all of which you have the power to change.

This book will provide you with the right tools and exercises you need to start to make that shift. You will learn exactly what thoughts, feelings, and actions are tripping you up and learn just what to do to set yourself on a course towards greater social confidence. The program that you will be going through in this book is the same program we use to help men just like you break through long standing shyness and social anxiety at The Center for Social Confidence. Some of them have been shy their entire lives and have never had a date or been in a relationship. Some are so scared to start a conversation that they get panic attacks just from imagining it.

After learning the material in this book, and doing the exercises, they are able to overcome crippling shyness and social anxiety to create satisfying friendships, enjoy rich and fulfilling relationships, and pursue the career and life goals that are most meaningful to them. No matter how long you have struggled with shyness, or how severe your social anxiety, it is possible for you to take action that will help you improve.

Even if that seems like an unbelievable stretch to you now, I encourage you to keep reading. You do not have to believe it yet. All I am asking is that you remain open to the possibility that your life can be different. To hold it as possible that you can learn new ideas, new skills, and new approaches that will shift your experience and help you get more of what you want out of life.

SHYNESS AND SOCIAL ANXIETY

Despite what our culture might say, there is nothing wrong with being shy. In a different era, or in different cultures, being quiet, humble, and respectful of others were and remain highly valued traits. However in our current competitive western culture, being bold, taking charge and being confident are heralded as ideal traits. Being shy is often synonymous with being timid or weak. This is unfortunate, because many people who feel shy or anxious around others already fear and assume that people will judge and criticize them. If you believe that there is something wrong with you for being shy, then you feel even worse about yourself.

The purpose of this book is to help you see that there is nothing wrong with you. It is to help you see where you are stuck or struggling, and to turn towards your challenges with compassion and acceptance. The goal is not to become permanently confident and to never feel scared again, or to eradicate shyness forever. That is unrealistic and discounts that the same trait of shyness also makes you kinder, more patient, and a better listener.

The real goal is to look at the areas of your life where you feel limited and stuck by feelings of shyness. When you feel like you cannot do the things in your life that really matter to you, such as finding a job that satisfies you, or creating a loving relationship with a beautiful partner, then it is time to do something about your shyness. When shyness prevents you from living the life that you truly want, then it can be described as social anxiety or social phobia. This simply means that in certain areas your shyness is negatively impacting your life and causing you distress.

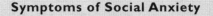

Symptoms of Social Anxiety

- You feel extremely uncomfortable in social situations and often avoid them.
- You are frequently worried that other people are judging you negatively.
- You are hyper self-conscious and always watching what you say or do so you don't say the "wrong" thing.
- You find rejection or disapproval intolerable and do whatever you can to avoid it.
- You often feel like others are watching you and you constantly avoid doing anything embarrassing.
- You can feel worried or anxious for days or even weeks before a challenging situation.
- You regularly criticize and judge yourself for feeling anxious.
- Your anxiety, worry, and avoidance significantly interfere with your life.
- You may feel hopeless about your situation, angry at yourself, or angry at others.

BEWARE OF LABELING YOURSELF

Reading the above section can be helpful in identifying some of your struggles with feeling tense or anxious around others. The term "social anxiety" gives you a shorthand way to refer to your experience. Social anxiety is not something that you are, and it is not some defect or disease. It is an experience of feeling pain or discomfort around others that comes from patterns of thinking and feeling.

A common question is whether people are born with social anxiety. Psychological research on infants has found that some people are born with more of what researchers call *behavioral inhibition*. This means they are less extroverted and tend to be more easily over-stimulated by high levels of interaction. While this inhibition can be seen as a form of shyness, it does not directly lead to social anxiety.

Social anxiety is a complex result of many experiences from your environment growing up—your biology, your family, your early childhood experiences, your experiences in grade school, middle school, high school, etc. These stages of development help us learn more about the world around us, and ourselves. It is during these years that we make conclusions about ourselves, such as *people don't like me,* or *I am not good enough,* which create social anxiety.

Therefore social anxiety is not something that you are just born with and stuck with for your entire life, and it is not who you are. It is a pattern of thoughts and feelings that you learned somewhere along the way—which means it can be unlearned. Identifying yourself as a "socially anxious" person is useful if it helps you to have compassion and patience with yourself as you learn and grow. It is not useful if you use it as a conclusion and a reason to give up or avoid taking action.

Limited Options, Limited Satisfaction

If you've been dealing with shyness for a while, then your choices regarding whom you talk to, what you can say, where you can go, and what you can do feel pretty limited. If your experience of meeting new people is frequently one of discomfort, awkwardness, and embarrassment, then most likely you avoid putting yourself in that situation. If you hate going to bars or parties, then you naturally do not go to those either. How do you deal with this?

The first step to breaking through limiting shyness and social fears is to become more aware of what your fears are and how you respond to them. This awareness is the first step to shifting your patterns.

Remember the scenario described earlier where you are meeting someone new and you have nothing to say? If we were to turn that situation into a multiple-choice question, what would your options be?

You have just met someone new and exchanged names. You are both standing there looking at each other. No one has said anything yet. What do you do?

a. Blurt out a random comment, such as "Boy, it's sure been raining a lot, huh?"
b. Stare wide-eyed at the other person until they say something.
c. Wait for their lead, then nod and agree with what they are saying.
d. Give an excuse and exit the situation.

These are the most common options that we choose from when we are feeling anxious around others. None of these options is particularly satisfying. In fact, not only are they unfulfilling socially, each one actually has a downside that makes you feel worse afterwards. The second part of this book will help you see that you have much more satisfying options, and help you develop the courage and self-confidence to choose them. In the meantime, what option do you typically choose? What is your default?

Each response is worth examining briefly. Doing so will highlight the fact that none of them will give you what you truly want when connecting with others. As this becomes clearer, you will be able to learn new patterns that will increase your enjoyment of meeting new people and being around others.

Option A: "Sure been raining a lot, huh?"

Blurting something out can sometimes get the ball rolling in the conversation. In fact, as we will discuss later in this book, turning down your filter and blurting things out can actually help your social life. However, saying something you are not really interested in—just to say something, anything—is the problem. This kind of comment is hard to respond to and often does not spark interesting conversation. This can then kick your mind into an even higher gear: *What the hell was that? Sure been raining a lot? Idiot! You're so awkward. What the hell is wrong with you? She thinks you're a freak. Look at you just standing there.*

Now you are not only trying to start a conversation with someone you do not know, you are attacking yourself in your head. This can be incredibly distracting, can make thinking of something to say even harder, and can make you feel terrible about yourself.

Option B—Stare wide-eyed and wait

This option is not much better than A. For one, while you are waiting there, your mind can launch wave after wave of distracting and painful self-attack. Even when the other person does say something, you might be too distracted by your inner critic to respond effectively. Once your mind starts to become self-conscious and self-critical, it can be very challenging to remain present and spontaneous in a conversation.

Option C—Nod and agree with everything they say

Once the conversation is going, most shy people will choose option C. This involves being very agreeable, nice, friendly, and non-offensive. You nod as they are speaking, laugh at their jokes, and are sure to say things that you know they will like. Most shy people are highly intuitive and socially aware, so you are most likely able to guess accurately what the person wants to hear.

This was my default option for many years, and I notice I still fall back into this pattern when I am feeling nervous around someone. In the next chapter we will discuss why this option is one of the most common defaults when you are feeling shy. When you do not really like yourself, you tend to modify your behavior to get the approval you need from others.

At this point you might be thinking: Well what's wrong with option C? Isn't it good to be friendly, ask them questions about themselves, and avoid offensive topics?

In response to those questions, I have a question for you. How do you feel after an interaction like that? Are you satisfied, happy, fulfilled? Do you feel connected to that person and energized? Or do you feel uncomfortable, nervous, irritated or sad? Were you really interested in the conversation, or were you bored? Do you feel fulfilled and eager to connect with that person again, or do you feel tired and drained? Do you dread having more social interactions?

Many shy people I work with experience these feelings after being social. And many of them are choosing option C when interacting with others. While being warm, interested, and friendly are fantastic ways to connect with others, when feeling shy we often do this out of fear rather than genuine interest. We are also scared to share too much about ourselves, making the interaction one-sided and ultimately unfulfilling.

If you see yourself in option C, congratulations! Gaining awareness is an absolutely essential step in creating lasting change. In the next section you will learn exactly why you choose option C again and again, even though it might not be completely satisfying. Then you will learn how to shift out of this pattern and into one that leaves you feeling happy and excited after social interactions.

Option D—Give an excuse and exit

This option is possibly the most common default, along with playing nice, nodding, and being overly friendly. In fact, when feeling social anxiety, many of us will go one step further and actually avoid the interaction entirely. This allows you to side-step the pain and embarrassment of that awkward conversation.

When we are feeling shy or anxious around people, it is very easy to develop many layers of avoidance. While this provides an immediate relief in the short term, it can actually worsen shyness over time and can leave you feeling unfulfilled and lonely. One level of avoidance is to immediately end the conversation as quickly as possible. Many people I work with say they often do this when speaking with someone they find attractive.

Shy Quote:

I don't know why I keep doing this, but as soon as a woman I'm interested in starts talking to me, I have a strong desire to flee the situation. I become tense, cold, and unresponsive and just keep looking for a way out. Then afterwards I beat myself up for not being more confident.

Noticing your desire to avoid the uncomfortable situations is a key step in breaking the patterns of shyness. As you will see later in this book, the primary pathway to a life of lasting confidence and trust in yourself is to steadily and regularly step outside of your "comfort zone." This involves doing things that you used to avoid, and approaching what scares you in social interactions. At first, this might feel incredibly uncomfortable, like jumping off the high dive at a pool. However, over time you will start to see that you get accustomed to trying new things, and that what once scared you no longer seems so intimidating.

Before embarking on that journey, however, it is essential that you have a clear understanding of why you would choose any of these unfulfilling options in the first place. All of these choices are the result of feeling afraid and anxious during a social inter-action. Why do we get anxious in the first place?

WHAT MAKES YOU ANXIOUS?

Let's take a moment to look directly at your life and the areas where you feel stuck or held back due to social fears. We will go through a brief process that will help you identify your most challenging areas. Later in the book, we will help you use this information to create your unique action plan to break through your shyness.

What follows is a list of situations where people can feel shy or socially anxious. Take a moment to scan the list. Next to each sit-uation, write a number between 1 and 10 to indicate the amount of anxiety or fear you would feel during that activity or situation:

A "1" means you would feel no fear whatsoever.
A "5" indicates a moderate amount of nervousness and fear.
A "7" or "8" means your heart would be pounding in your chest.
A "10" means you would be *terrified* to be in this situation.

In addition to writing a number that corresponds with each ac-tivity or situation, take a moment to ask yourself, "how much do I avoid this situation?" This is an important question, because if you avoid a situation regularly, you might not feel much fear.

When I was doing this exercise with a client recently, we were looking at situation 7 below: *Approach two women to start a conversation.* He paused to think about it, then said he would give it a 4. This surprised me, since he rated *Approaching a wom-an sitting by herself in a coffee shop* an 8.

As we discussed the situation more, I discovered he rated it a 4 because he had avoided doing anything like this his entire life, and could never see himself even considering doing anything like it. When our avoidance is very high in an area, we may actually feel less anxious because we know we would never put ourselves in that situation. In that way, we have effectively checked out from the possibility.

Therefore, when ranking the situations below, actually imagine yourself doing them, even if they are things you have checked out from, and would never consider doing.

Situation	Fear (1-10)
1. Going to a party or social gathering	
2. Speaking or performing in front of an audience	
3. Eating alone in public	
4. Going to the movie theater alone	
5. Calling someone you don't know very well	
6. Approaching a woman sitting by herself in a coffee shop	
7. Approaching two women to start a conversation	
8. Meeting someone new	
9. Speaking up in a group of people	
10. Dancing while sober	
11. Having a conversation with someone you don't know very well	

12. Urinating in a public bathroom	
13. Being the center of attention	
14. Disagreeing with someone you don't know very well	
15. Letting a woman know you are interested in her sexually	
16. Complimenting a stranger	
17. Asking a woman out	
18. Clearly and directly expressing anger or annoyance to the person you are upset with	
19. Other: (write in your own)	
20. Other: (write in your own)	

Knowing which situations tend to make you anxious, and how much you tend to avoid these situations is incredibly valuable. At first it can seem overwhelming—*look at all these areas where I get anxious. My god, what's wrong with me??*

Actually, even though you may feel anxious across dozens of situations, there is just one underlying factor that connects them all. Once you clearly see and understand this underlying belief, you can start to shift your experience. As you do this, you will notice a decrease in anxiety across all situations.

Two

THE CORE OF IT ALL

Why are we so uncomfortable and fearful around other people? What could possibly make us feel this way? This fear can show up in virtually any social situation. Worse still, it can start long before you are even around people, and continue long after the situation is over.

Have you ever had to give a talk or presentation in front of a group? Did you find yourself getting tense and anxious days ahead of time? And even after you managed to get through it, you were still not free. You might have experienced several more days of reliving the experience, seeing all the awkward moments again and again.

I remember when I first started teaching weekend courses at a university, I would be absolutely *terrified* in the week leading up to the class. I would feel a sense of dread, anxiety, and an increase in my insecurities in all areas of life. When the weekend finally arrived and I began speaking with the students, I noticed a tendency to focus on the one or two students who seemed the least interested. Even if forty other students seemed engaged, I would be focused on the two who didn't seem to like me or want to be there. For days after the weekend, I couldn't get the image of those students shaking their heads in disapproval out of my mind.

As you identified earlier, there can be dozens of unique situations or activities that make you feel uncomfortable. You might grit your teeth, push yourself, and endure some of them as I did when I first started teaching. Other situations you might avoid entirely. While it may seem like dozens of different situations cause anxiety, there is actually just one single factor underlying all your discomfort. Whether it is meeting strangers, getting to know someone new, or having dinner alone in a restaurant, all of your social fears can be distilled down to one primary fear.

THE PRIMARY FEAR

For some it is strong, persistent, always there. For others, the fear strikes infrequently and intermittently, but remains powerful: on some deep level, I am not something enough as a person.

I am not smart enough.
I am not good-looking enough.
I am not attractive enough.
I am not strong enough.
I am not clever enough.
I am not successful enough.
I am not motivated enough.
I am not rich enough.

And because I am not enough in this way, I will not be loved. People will not accept me. They will judge me, mock me, and reject me. I will lose connection and be isolated and alone.

When we feel like there is something wrong with us, that we are not worthy of love and belonging, we can describe this feeling as *shame*.[1] It is the sense that you are somehow inadequate, bad, inferior or defective. It is a terribly uncomfortable feeling that everyone knows and nobody likes.

---

1. This is an adaptation of Brene Brown's definition of shame. She has done groundbreaking research on the subject in her books, including *I Thought It Was Just Me* (New York: Penguin Group, 2007).

Shy Quote:
I get this hollow, heavy, sinking feeling right in the center of my chest. It feels like everything is collapsing into this hole and I just want to sink into the earth.

The feeling of shame is so painful that we will often do anything we can to avoid it. A major difficulty in social anxiety, however, is that we frequently feel like we are not good enough. This has been described as *toxic shame.*[2]

Toxic shame describes the tendency to feel shame much of the time, even when you have not done anything particularly bad. You regularly believe that there is something wrong with you and that others will reject you because of it. As a human, this is a terrifying prospect because love is a primary need. Infants and children who do not receive enough affection and love are actually at physical risk of death due to a syndrome that has been dubbed "Failure to Thrive." This occurs in scenarios where children do not receive a bare minimum of nurturance, touch, and love. This tragic outcome for some children clearly demonstrates just how deep and primal our need for love is.

Behavioral psychologists have conducted research with infant primates to determine which need is more primary—love or food. In one experiment researchers presented a baby monkey with a choice—it could either get milk from a bottle that was held by cold, abrasive wire mesh in the shape of a mother monkey, or it could snuggle with a soft, fuzzy mother monkey doll that had no milk. Consistently, the baby monkey chose the comforting, soft fur over the food.

---

2. This concept is described in more detail in Robert Glover's book *No More Mr. Nice Guy* (Philadelphia: Barnes & Noble Publishing, 2003).

We are social creatures. We value love and connection above all else. The idea that we are not going to receive love because of some defect in ourselves can cause a tremendous amount of fear and anxiety. This fear can cause us to be nervous around others. *What if they see that there is something wrong with me?*

This fear causes us to be wary of how we come across, and to be extremely self-conscious while interacting with others. It leads to a need to hide flaws and character defects, for fear of being "found out" and rejected. When we are feeling socially anxious, we essentially feel like we are on a narrow tightrope above a 200 foot drop. The slightest false move will bring on harsh judgment, ridicule and rejection.

SEEING YOUR CORE BELIEF

The primary fear that something is wrong with us—and therefore others will not like us—is often not fully conscious. You might not literally be thinking this when you are nervous. Instead, you may just feel tense or jittery. You might just avoid the conversation or try to find a way to exit the interaction once it has started.

Beneath this fear—and the associated discomfort—lies a deep, core belief. More than just a thought, it is something you can feel deep in your chest, solar plexus, and stomach. To see for yourself what your core belief is, let us use an example that often brings about discomfort and shame, even for those who do not consider themselves shy.

Imagine you are in a supermarket and you see a woman you are attracted to in the produce aisle. She is just your type, and you get excited and nervous just glancing at her. You are currently single, and are looking to meet someone to spend time with. This is *the perfect opportunity*. What do you do?

For many guys, this situation is in the 7-to-10 anxiety range. There is no way in hell they would go over and start a conversation. What are the most common reasons? First, take a second to think of your own. How would you stop yourself from going over to start a conversation?

Top 10 Reasons to NOT Start a Conversation

1. That would be weird.
2. She would think I was hitting on her (and be annoyed).
3. She will be freaked out.
4. Other people will see me get rejected (and judge me).
5. I don't have anything good to say.
6. She's probably in a relationship already.
7. She's out of my league.
8. I don't have enough money, what could I offer her?
9. She wouldn't want to be with a guy like me.
10. It will go terribly wrong and then I'll feel embarrassed and awful for the rest of the week.

Usually, this barrage of self-criticism and negative predictions is enough to stop us from taking a chance. What do these thoughts say about how you see yourself? They can all be boiled down to one simple belief: *I'm not good enough for her, and she will reject me.*

The idea is that if someone were to see you for who you are, as you are, it would be impossible for them to truly like you because you are in fact somehow, on a deep level, revolting or unlovable. This core belief lurks behind every social interaction in which you are nervous, scared, self-critical or awkward. Once you are able to see this, you can start taking steps to shift this belief, which will cause a cascade of changes across all your social interactions.

JEFF'S STORY—I'M NOT NORMAL

Jeff, a 23-year-old college student, came to see me because he had an intense fear of interacting with people. The tipping point that led him to seek help came after some classmates he barely knew invited him to dinner. Sick and tired of feeling shy and avoiding opportunities, he decided to accept the invitation and meet them at the restaurant. Leading up to the dinner he spent days thinking, worrying, and planning every aspect of the meal. *What will I wear? I should look at the menu ahead of time so I can look like I know the place. What if I run out of things to say?*

What made matters more challenging was that Jeff had an interest in Sarah, one of the women in the group. He had only spoken with her once, but he had been attracted to her for quite some time. He spent hours wondering what he could say or do that would get her to like him. He spent many more hours telling himself that he was an idiot and that she was way more interested in the taller, stronger, more athletic guys that were all over campus. *Who am I kidding? She is way out of my league.*

On the day of the dinner Jeff felt sick most of the afternoon. He could not eat his lunch, nor could he focus in his classes. He started to feel more and more anxious, and then had an idea that gave him an incredible sense of relief: *I could just call and say that I'm sick.*

While this option did help him relax a little, Jeff was determined not to back out from this one. He let go of the desire to flee and resolved to go to dinner no matter what.

He arrived at the restaurant several minutes early. He felt incredibly self-conscious standing around waiting for them, and he hated the idea of being at a table alone waiting for them to arrive. He decided to go into the bathroom and wash his hands to kill some time. Inside the bathroom he turned on the faucet and began to wash his hands in the cold stream of water. He looked at his reflection in the mirror while his mind raced.

You can't do this. There's no way. You have nothing to talk about. Your face looks terrible. You can see leftover scars from your acne and dark circles around your eyes. You can't do this. Who do you think you are?

As these thoughts raced through his mind he began to feel more and more frightened. His heart started beating like a jack-hammer in his chest and the room became slightly blurry. His hands started tingling and he found it hard to get a full breath. *What the hell is happening to me?* Just as he asked that question he heard footsteps coming towards the bathroom door. The thought of someone else seeing him like this sent another wave of panic through his already terrified nervous system.

He turned off the water and dashed into a nearby stall and closed the door. Inside the stall he felt slightly safer—at least no one would see him. Jeff stayed in the stall for 15 minutes. He started to calm down slightly, but his shirt was soaked in sweat. He was 10 minutes late for the dinner and probably looked like hell. *What am I going to do?*

When Jeff told me this story, he paused at this point and looked up. He had been gazing down at the floor as he recounted his experience, feeling embarrassed and ashamed.

"I couldn't do it. I just left. I walked straight out of the bathroom and made a b-line for the door. I don't know if they saw me. I didn't make eye contact, I didn't call to tell them I couldn't make it, I didn't do anything. I ruined that chance just like I ruin every chance I get."

He paused and tapped his fingers against his leg and looked back down at the gray carpet. "There's something wrong with me. I'm not normal. No one else experiences this much fear about meeting some new people."

THE CAUSE OF SHYNESS

The idea that you are somehow insufficient, not enough, broken or damaged is the major source of social anxiety. It has a profound effect on how you see yourself, and how willing you are to let others see your real self. This one idea will significantly impact every area of your life. It will determine whether you approach a stranger, how close you let your partner get to you in a relationship, and even whether you allow yourself to have a relationship to begin with. It will affect your work life, job, career choices and level of financial success. This idea is at the center of shyness and social anxiety. It is, in fact, the *cause* of social anxiety.

This *I am not enough* idea is not unique to people who are shy or socially anxious. In fact, most people in our culture struggle with feelings of inadequacy. This is part of growing up in a media-saturated environment full of messages implying we are somehow insufficient. The difference between someone who has social anxiety and someone who does not can be distilled down to one thing: those with the anxiety believe more completely, and more frequently, that they are not enough. That is the crux of social anxiety.

What about the source of this idea? For many, the information that they are not good enough was initially conveyed by the world around them when they were younger. Indeed, if you have social anxiety, it's highly likely that you had negative experiences in childhood involving neglect, abuse, criticism, or ridicule from family members and/or peers. Such experiences created and reinforced the idea that you were somehow not good enough, and taught you that you need to strive to be better, avoid making mistakes, and work hard to get people to like you.

Regardless of who first conveyed to you that you are not good enough, in the present moment, *you are now your biggest critic.* You have taken the negative messages from others and *internalized* them, making them part of yourself. At this point in your life, you are the one who is repeatedly reinforcing that belief on a daily basis, and re-conditioning yourself to feel that you are not enough.

BELIEVING IS SEEING

We reinforce the "I am not enough" idea through consistently repeating certain thoughts and ideas in our minds throughout the day. We focus on what could go wrong, how social interactions could be awkward, and why people will probably not like us. We see images in our minds of tense and awkward moments, of ourselves acting in an embarrassing or unattractive way. Most importantly, we avoid taking risks to see if our worst fears are actually true. We just assume they are and act accordingly. We pass up opportunities, refuse to try, or make half-hearted attempts. Our minds then reinforce our worst fears by concluding: *See, I knew they wouldn't like me.*

In a sense we are running a propaganda campaign against ourselves. In the section about your inner critic you will learn much more about this internal campaign against yourself. For now it is important to see how your mind, on a daily basis, is convincing you of the primary belief that you are inadequate. It is reinforced in our thoughts dozens of times per day, and plastered on the walls of our minds. With all of this repetition, this idea can start to seem more and more convincing. It also blocks out new information from the outside that might provide alternative evidence: *Perhaps not everyone will reject me. Maybe she could actually find me attractive. Maybe she'll be nervous to talk with me!*

But this does not fit with the propaganda story, so we immediately discount it. Our minds have an incredible capacity to find what we are looking for. If we are looking for evidence that we are not enough and that other people will not like us, then we will find it. We will even create this evidence when none exists.

To illustrate this, let's try a little experiment. When you finish this paragraph, take a moment to look around the room and count everything you can see that is red. Scan around you in all directions. Make sure you look behind you as well. Count everything red you can see. Do this for 10 seconds. Begin now.

Good. Now, without looking away from this page, read the following sentence and do what it says:

Close your eyes and think of everything you saw that was *green*.

How many green items did you notice when you were searching for red? Two? One? Zero? When your brain is searching for red, it finds red and completely ignores green. Even more interesting, did you find things that were *kind of red* and count them as red?

Our minds do the exact same thing when searching for evidence as to why we are not good enough. It fixates on finding the evidence that supports the idea that we are not good enough. In research psychology, this is called a *confirmation bias*. It describes how we tend to find evidence to support our hunch, and ignore the evidence that contradicts it.

Not only do we search for confirming evidence, we tend to take anything that is *close enough* and count that as evidence as well. If a person looks down while we were talking, that is close enough to a sign of rejection and is counted as such. After all, the material in a propaganda campaign does not have to be *true*. It just has to be repeated loud enough, long enough, and consistently enough and it will become convincing through repetition alone.

Research conducted on people with social anxiety shows that they are indeed searching for red. In studies where researchers show people pictures on a computer screen of other people's faces, those without social anxiety tend to look at the whole face. They start by looking at the other person's eyes, then the nose and mouth, and then around to the cheeks, jaw, forehead and other areas. People who are shy and anxious start by looking at the other person's eyes, then they hyper-focus on two primary areas: the innermost portion of the eyebrows and the corners of the mouth. They are searching for lowering of the eyebrows, which is an expression of anger, and curling of the corners of the mouth, which can indicate disdain or disgust. In short, socially anxious people actively search for ways that others might be upset or disapproving of them. What we seek we shall…

KNOWING THE CAUSE POINTS YOU TOWARDS THE SOLUTION

There are many things that come together to contribute to the challenge you face with social anxiety and debilitating shyness. You may have been born with a more sensitive nervous system, or a tendency towards shyness. Psychologists who conduct personality research with infants call this *behavioral inhibition*. You may have had many negative experiences in your past that confirmed that you were not enough, that you were deficient, defective, or unlovable. Whether it was a parent frequently yelling at you, or other kids in middle school making fun of you, this message may have been conveyed hundreds of times.

While these historical experiences have a strong impact on your challenges now, they are no longer the *source* of your social anxiety. Reflecting on these experiences from the past can be helpful in developing understanding and compassion for yourself. However, doing so might not entirely liberate you from your social fears because these historical events are not the *current source* of your difficulties. The current source of your social anxiety, the current cause of the problem that affects you every time you leave your house, is the belief that you are not enough—a belief that is reinforced throughout each moment of your day.

This belief stops you from speaking with strangers, from seeing yourself as worthwhile and lovable, and from feeling at ease in your own skin. All those events from the past may have helped instill and sustain the belief, but now it is something you are actively reinforcing on a daily basis. Realizing this takes the problem out of the realm of something we can do nothing about (the past), and places it into the realm of something we can change (our beliefs about ourselves).

You are continually reconstructing your perception of yourself. The more clearly you see how you are actively creating an identity that does not serve you, the more you will be able to take action toward shifting this toxic story about yourself.

WHAT IS TO COME

The first part of this book is designed to help you increase your awareness of the inner workings of shyness. This is an essential component of change, as you will see in the pages to come. The second part of this book is dedicated to teaching you exactly how to shift this old toxic belief that you are not enough. It will give you the ideas, tools, exercises, guidance, and support to help challenge this belief and to find a new, empowering way to see yourself in the world.

As you do this, your fear of other people will start to diminish. The world will start to appear less scary, and other people less intimidating. Instead of a hostile environment where others will despise you for your vulnerability, mistakes, and humanness, the world will start to appear more inviting, more adventurous, and friendlier. That sense of always being on the edge of rejection will begin to dissolve. You will start to feel and know on a deep level that the world is safe in many ways, that people are generally friendly, and that people generally like you and want what is best for you. If someone does not like you, then you have the ability to respond to him or her with assertiveness, by setting a boundary, or by distancing yourself. You have many options to deal with the parts of the world that are unsafe, and for the most part, you do not need to live in fear of other people.

Helping you shed your fear of other people is the whole point of this program. To make sure you are no longer frightened of their judgments, dislikes or rejection. To help you have the self-esteem to reveal who you are, what you are about, your thoughts, your feelings, your experience—the vulnerable, authentic you that you value and hold dear. This will allow you to form deep connections where people know the real you. As you gain the courage to be more vulnerable with those around you, trusting that they will receive you with kindness and curiosity, you might start to see how everyone has their own fears and flaws.

If you are going to conclude that you are defective, or broken, or not enough, then you might start to see that everyone else is as well. We are all imperfect, flawed humans doing the best we can with our given resources at the time. The struggles you think make you uniquely worse than others are in fact not so unique. Carl Jung had a saying that the more personal an experience is, the more universal it is. You just might find there are more people than you think who are dealing with these very same challenges.

Shyness and social anxiety really come down to how much someone has bought into the belief that he or she is not enough. This belief is strongly present in our culture. It is floating around in our parents, our bosses, our churches, our schools. It permeates our magazines, televisions, and movies. It is in the very air we breathe. The only difference between you and someone who you consider "normal" is this one belief. You have taken it in, just like everyone else, but you believe it more intensely and more frequently than others might.

For example, someone else might believe it 25% of the time while you believe it 95% of the time. Do you think the most confident, outgoing, incredibly good looking, desirable, wealthy person in the world never feels insecure? Never gets worried? Is never anxious? He never feels embarrassed or afraid of what other people are going to think of him? Of course he does, but maybe he just feels that way 10% of the time. In truth, there is no fundamental difference between you and someone else. You simply believe something more often and more completely. It is entirely possible for you to shift this belief, perhaps more rapidly than you realize.

That said, the skills and exercises in this book take time to learn and practice, and the process of growing confidence is ongoing. There is no immediate, permanent cure or quick fix. It is a lifelong process of getting to know ourselves better, developing compassion for ourselves, and learning how to take healthy risks while managing our fears and doubts. While the process of creating more confidence is ongoing, the *willingness* to shift this belief happens in a moment. All it takes is a moment of doubt. *Maybe it is just a belief, an idea that I've had for a long time. Maybe there is nothing wrong with me…*Once that doubt exists, you will be able to apply the skills outlined in this book, take the necessary risks, and get evidence from the world around you that you are, in fact, lovable.

Usually, the shift does not happen until you put in the hard work of taking new actions in the world. It would be really nice if by reading something your core belief could simply switch, but in my experience it takes new actions and behaviors. It requires doing things that are uncomfortable, that you might not want to do at first. When you are first starting out, you might not feel like you are a complete, lovable, and attractive person *before* you go talk to someone. You might be terrified and convinced that they will reject you. This is a normal and natural part of the process. All you have to be at this point is *willing* to try an experiment. To interact with the world and really test it by asking yourself: *Is my certainty that I will get rejected really true?*

You just might find that your belief is actually not true, that the person actually does not reject you. As you repeat this kind of experiment again and again, you will accumulate a growing body of evidence that shows you that you are indeed worthy of love and belonging. As this evidence grows, it eventually becomes harder and harder to believe in the old story that you are not enough and that you are not lovable.

To that end, let us turn towards the hallmark fear of social anxiety—being rejected by others.

REJECTION SENSITIVITY

WHAT WILL THEY THINK OF ME?

Do you frequently ask yourself this question? For most people struggling with shyness, this question is foremost in their minds. In fact, fear of others judging and scrutinizing you is the hallmark of social anxiety. Remember that social anxiety comes from believing on some level that you are not good enough and therefore not worthy of love and belonging. When you believe this, you will feel anxious around others. Believing this will also make you hyper-sensitive to rejection from others, because it confirms that deep fear inside of you.

Often times when I am working with someone, they will become frustrated and upset with their fear of what others will think of them.

Shy Quote:
I hate how nervous I get around people I don't even know. I go to the store and I'm walking down the aisle and I'm constantly thinking about how I look to all the other people in that aisle. Am I walking upright? Do I look stiff and unnatural? What the hell is wrong with me? Why do I care so much about what people I don't even know think of me?

If you have had this experience, you know how frustrating it can be. You also know how hard it can be to shake that concern about what others think of you. However, despite being uncomfortable or frustrating, this fear makes complete sense. If you are convinced there is something wrong with you, and that once people see or realize this they will not want anything to do with you, of course you would feel self-conscious!

Being rejected, cast out, and otherwise ousted from the pack is a deeply primal fear in all humans. We are social animals. The loss of connection with the group is a primary threat. As such, your mind is going to be very aware of anything that might bring this about and will and label it as dangerous. Worse still, once you buy into the idea that you are *somehow defective and not lovable,* then you perceive it as inevitable that, sooner or later, you will make a mistake, and the group will kick you out.

How does this fear impact you on a daily basis? Is it something you notice only when meeting new people or approaching a stranger? Is it something you feel all the time? Does it even affect you when no other people are around, just from imagining what others would think if they saw what you were doing or knew what you were thinking? For most people with social anxiety, there is no escape, only the perpetual sense of fear of rejection. Thus, any connection with others can feel very fragile. *Sure, they like me today, but if I'm not happy and upbeat all the time, then they will eventually not want to be around me.*

WHY REJECTION HURTS SO MUCH

When we ask, "What will other people think of me?" we are actually saying, "I hope they do not have judgmental or critical thoughts of me." If you are feeling particularly anxious, you might be thinking: *They think I look ridiculous, they think I'm an idiot.* In this case, you have already concluded that they are judging you negatively. What happens when someone thinks negatively of us? That person will have negative feelings towards us—anger, irritation, annoyance, disapproval, disgust, etc.

The reason this can be so painful, especially when we are shy, is because we make it completely about us. For example, if you are at work and your co-worker John indicates he does not approve of something you just said, it can be all too easy to conclude: *John sees that I'm stupid and inconsiderate and has good reason to disapprove of me. I am bad, not good enough, and don't deserve to be liked.*

Instead of being curious about what is going on with John, you immediately conclude that there is something wrong with you. It is not that you have a difference of opinion and John disagrees with you, or that John might have some personal reaction that does not have much to do with you. You do not attribute it to John at all. You attribute it to yourself and assume that John is really seeing the real, flawed person that you are.

Why is rejection so painful to us when we are shy? This sensitivity is due to each rejection feeling like confirmation of the inherent worthlessness of you as a person. To see this in action, think of the last time you felt rejected. This could have been during a conversation, with a group, in a meeting, or anywhere else where someone might have indicated they did not like something you said or did. Can you think of a moment like that?

After that experience, what did you say to yourself in your mind? Usually it is some version of: *God that was ridiculous! What's wrong with me? I was so awkward and embarrassing! No wonder she didn't like you. You sounded so nervous and pathetic.*

This harsh criticism, which can be a constant companion for those with social anxiety, regularly highlights why you are not good enough and not worthy of love. We will go into great detail in the second part of this book about how to deal with this internal critic so you can start encouraging and supporting yourself. In the meantime, can you see how each rejection becomes further evidence that you are somehow inadequate? This evidence is then used against you, saying you are not worthy of friendship, connection, or love. Worst of all, because the problem is inside of you and apparently permanent, you will *never* have connection and love with someone you really desire. That incredibly painful thought makes rejection intolerable.

Fortunately, it is not true. As you read further and start to do some of the social experiments, you will discover that these are simply *beliefs* you hold about yourself and about rejection. As you shift these beliefs and start having new experiences, you will find that rejection stops being an all-encompassing and overwhelming experience that triggers strong self-loathing. Instead, you will learn how to tolerate rejection, how to strengthen yourself to the inevitable rejections you will face on your path towards success. As you apply the strategies in this book, you will become *inoculated* to rejection and it will no longer cripple you or hold you back.

AVOIDING REJECTION

We humans are very intelligent creatures. If something causes us pain, we tend to avoid it. Few experiences are more painful for humans than the feeling of being worthless and unloved. If some behavior or experience causes you to feel like you are deeply flawed and worthless, then most likely you will avoid whatever causes this experience. This is exactly what most of us do with rejection. It is uncomfortable, painful, embarrassing, and discouraging, so we do whatever we can to avoid it. The cost of this strategy, however, is quite high. What happens if you avoid all forms of rejection? What happens when you avoid all risk?

Almost anything worth having requires taking some measure of risk. Whether it is applying for your top school, approaching a woman you find fascinating, going in for the kiss, putting yourself out there, going for the dream job, or pursuing a career that fills you with passion, you will inevitably encounter rejections along the way. *Many* rejections.

We will discuss how to transform your relationship to fear and rejection in the second part of this book. First, it is important to see the ways in which you tend to avoid risk and rejection. This will help you gain awareness of your patterns, which is an essential first step to applying the strategies you will learn later on.

Avoidance Strategy 1: Basic avoidance

The primary way of trying to avoid rejection is basic avoidance. It is fairly straightforward: *If I avoid the thing that is going to reject me then I will not get rejected.*

This type of avoidance is almost a default, and we might do it dozens of times per day. Whether it involves approaching a girl to start a conversation, flirting with her, asking her out for a date, or taking her to a movie, we simply avoid anything that could lead to rejection. We avoid it because we do not want to feel any pain from rejection, which can directly poke that sensitive *I'm not good enough* spot.

Avoidance Strategy 2: Nice Guy

A slightly more sophisticated way of avoiding rejection is to become overly warm, friendly, agreeable, and "nice" to someone. This is different than being *genuinely* warm, open, and friendly, and it has a very different quality. Excessive niceness is born out of fear and is focused on saying and doing whatever we think we should in order to get the other person to like us. This can include being very friendly, nodding, and agreeing with whatever the other person says. We might smile and laugh at a joke, regardless of whether we found it funny or not.

One nice guy habit I had for years was to nod and agree with someone *even before they finished their sentence*. In fact, I would be agreeing with them even before I knew what they were actually saying!

Another form the nice guy avoidance strategy takes is excessive generosity. After all, if I give so much to them, how could they possibly reject me? While in some circumstances giving can feel incredibly good and lead to a mutually satisfying relationship, when giving comes from a place of fear and needing approval, *it almost never works*. This is because the giving is coming from a belief that *I am not enough and I must win you over with gifts because you would not love me for who I am*. This is a form of avoiding rejection, and rarely leads to a satisfying result. Even if the other person does not reject you, these kinds of social interactions are often one-sided and unfulfilling. Worst of all, they do not allow you to fully be yourself, which is essential for feeling connected and accepted in relationships.

It is important to note that there is nothing wrong with being nice, friendly, warm, or giving. People who are shy often have these valuable traits and strengths. The key is to realize the difference between genuine warmth and fear-based niceness. The latter is a way to avoid rejection and can limit your fulfillment in relationships.

Avoidance Strategy 3—Being aloof

A final way of avoiding rejection is through being detached or aloof. A common piece of feedback shy people often receive is that someone thinks they are disinterested, bored, or aloof. This strategy can involve a kind of dismissive quality in the way we interact with people. We do not say very much, or we might scoff or make a sarcastic remark in response to what someone is saying. We do not reveal much of ourselves, and we certainly are not vulnerable and open to the people around us. This is the flip side of the nice guy approach. The idea behind this strategy is *you are going to reject me, so I will reject you first.*

This is a way of protecting ourselves. If I have rejected you first and not shared much of myself with you, then if you reject me it will not affect me very much. The downside of this suit of armor is that it also blocks us from making satisfying connections with people who *will not* reject us.

BELIEF BECOMES BEHAVIOR

The more we ask ourselves what others think of us, the more we are unconsciously assuming they will reject us. This assumption keeps feeding the idea that we are not enough, deficient, or somehow flawed. When this belief is active, rejection becomes very painful, and it leads to a variety of behaviors.

Imagine you are at a bar with a friend and you see an attractive woman sitting at a nearby table with her friend. If you knew beyond a shadow of a doubt that she would reject you, would you go over and talk with her? Of course not! This belief causes you to stand there with your friend and order another drink. You may even talk about what you could say to her, or elbow your friend to encourage him to take the risk. Or, you might pretend like you do not really care, that she is not really that attractive, and that you would not want to spend time with the kind of woman who goes to a bar.

What if you believed that in order for her to like you, you had to be exactly what she wanted to *win her over?* If you believed this, you might go talk to her and be incredibly friendly, nice and over-accommodating. You might agree with everything she says, smile and nod. The next thing you know, she sees you as the *friend type.* Now you are in the *friend zone,* going shopping with her while she vents about the guy she is dating. There is *zero chance* she will ever be your girlfriend.

Can you see how your belief in this case directly affects what you will do?

Let's say you were absolutely certain, beyond a shadow of a doubt, that she found you attractive and was hoping you would come over and start a conversation. What would you do if you *knew* you could not fail? Your mind might be saying: *Well now, that's impossible. There is no way to know that and besides, there is absolutely no way someone like her could find someone like me attractive.*

Isn't it interesting how strong and convincing our beliefs can be? By the end of this book, if you have done the exercises and social experiments within, you will have a different perception of yourself. You will start to see how it is possible that beautiful women, and all other types of people, can and do find you attractive. For now, it is essential to realize that if your belief determines your behavior, then changing your beliefs will change your behavior. It will change what you are able to do in the world, and will change the results you experience.

Your Rejection Sensor

The fear of rejection is one of the most common experiences in shyness and social anxiety. Not only are we trying to avoid it at all costs, but also our internal sensors are finely attuned to it. When we feel some form of rejection, no matter how slight, it can have a harsh and all-encompassing quality to it.

When I was young, my family and I would take an annual trip to spend time with relatives in Los Angeles. Each time we visited, my cousins had a new word or phrase that was all the rage. One year it was "awesome" and the next it was *"budinksi."* Even if I didn't know what it meant, by the end of the week my brother and I were using the word of the summer in every other sentence.

One fateful summer, the word of the year was "rejected." Whenever my cousin would score a point in volleyball, tag you in "Marco Polo," or do anything that lead to a small victory for him, he would point his finger several inches from your face and yell, "RE-jected! Rejected! Rejected!"

At the time it was a disturbing and effective tactic that lead me to feel embarrassed. Looking back I find it quite ridiculous. It even puts a smile on my face. As ridiculous as it is, it captures the experience of what rejection feels like for those with social anxiety—like a full-body, wholesale dislike of you as a person, as if someone is standing in your face yelling "RE-jected!" over and over again.

ShyQuote:
I will never approach a girl if other people are around. I can handle her rejecting me, but if other people are close enough to listen in and hear me get rejected, I can't handle it. For the rest of the day I can't stop thinking about what a loser they think I am.

This quote highlights the way we can magnify rejection in our own minds. Rather than it being a passing occurrence that naturally happens when we take risks, we can blow rejection up to legendary status. Not only does the person who rejected us hate us, we assume that everyone will hear about this and naturally reject us as well. In cognitive therapy this is called the *brushfire fallacy*[3]—the assumption that once one person does something,

---

3. This cognitive distortion, as well as many others, is described in full detail in David Burns' *Intimate Connections* (New York: Penguin Group, 1985).

everyone else will follow suit like a dry prairie igniting from one small spark.

In addition to fearing that everyone will reject us, our rejection sensor can also exaggerate how others feel about us. If someone says "no, thanks," or "not right now," we can feel like they are saying "I hate you. You are pathetic. Go away." A simple "no" becomes complete revulsion. This sensitive rejection sensor leads to a heightened ability to perceive rejection around you. In conversations, you might be noticing and reacting to very subtle signs that indicate disapproval. Even though they are subtle, your sensor can pick up on them and it can feel just like someone is yelling "RE-jected!" in your face.

When our rejection sensors are set to pick up very subtle cues, we can feel rejected very frequently. You can feel rejected when someone is not interested in what you are saying, when someone has a slight disagreement with an idea of yours, or when someone does not want to hang out now and would prefer to hang out on a different day. Any of these subtle forms of disapproval can feel like a stab in the heart, an intensely uncomfortable or painful experience because they immediately plug into the *I'm not enough* self-concept.

I WANT *EVERYONE* TO LIKE ME

There is a Seinfeld episode in which George Costanza is becoming more and more agitated because Jerry's new girlfriend does not like him. He tries to reach out to her, to be more friendly with her, and even buys her a gift. As the episode progresses, he starts to become obsessed with how he can get her to like him. At one point Jerry breaks up with this girlfriend and she is storming out of his apartment, upset and hurting. George, who happens to be walking into the apartment at this exact moment, opens his mouth to speak to her. She brushes past him and cold-ly tells him to get out of her way.

After she walks out, George looks desperately at Jerry and says he is going to go after her. Seeing that George has no chance of reaching her, especially when she is so upset, Jerry asks, "George, does *every* single person have to like you?"

George pauses and reflects for a moment, then replies, "Yes. Every single person *has* to like me." He turns and runs out Jerry's door, pursuing the approval of a woman he does not even really know or particularly like.

When we are socially anxious and concerned that others will reject us because we are not good enough, we can find it in-tolerable that someone does not like us. Each person who does not approve of us is further evidence that we are not lovable.

The more we fear this, the more we worry that other people will realize our true, flawed nature and reject us as well. To compensate, we engage in a quest to make sure that everyone likes us. This can include listening to everyone, being friendly all of the time, doing whatever we think others would prefer, and generally being as accommodating as possible.

Unfortunately, this quest is a fool's errand and we will in-evitable fail. Somewhere along the line, someone will dislike something about us. When this happens, we can experience an onslaught of pain, fear, and self-rejection.

As you read on, you will discover how to free yourself of this need to make sure everyone likes you. As you do, you will discover who you really are, what you like, and how you want to interact with others once you are no longer afraid of their disapproval.

AVOIDING CONFLICT

Social anxiety can make experiencing any form of rejection so painful that we often end up avoiding anything that even feels like rejection. This often includes arguments, disagreements, and any form of conflict.

When we disagree with someone, or someone disagrees with us, it can feel tense, filled with feelings of mutual animosity and disapproval. When you have conflict with someone, you are inherently having some difference of opinions. They are not agreeing with or approving of some opinion, idea, or action of yours. This can feel like a rejection of you as a person, and can be uncomfortable and scary. It might even feel like this conflict is the beginning of the end of the relationship. While the fear of being rejected or abandoned is more acute when someone is yelling, or telling you they hate you, we can still feel it even with subtle disagreements.

Our fear of rejection makes us afraid of conflict, because any level of conflict feels threatening to the relationship. The first line of defense against conflict is *basic avoidance.*

- We do not mention things that bother us.
- We talk ourselves out of being bothered.
- We criticize ourselves in our heads for being "too sensitive."

If this does not work, we may take the second avoidance approach—being overly nice.

- We outwardly agree even when we inwardly disagree.
- We say whatever we need to in order to please the other person.
- We act in a more submissive and compliant manner.

Avoidance leads to a pattern of being that is not truly satisfying. If you are shy and uncomfortable with conflict, then you have experienced this. You end up selling yourself short, doing things you do not agree with, nodding and smiling, and taking the blame. You compromise your own desires and best interest in order to keep the peace. If you do have some sort of conflict, it feels like unbearable rejection. You might even harshly blame yourself for not being good enough to keep the other person from getting upset.

This way of relating is exhausting and extremely unrewarding. Worse still, you never show your *true self* around others. You never state your opinion clearly, stand up for yourself, or do the things that will create a greater sense of self-confidence. Stuffing down your opinions can lead to internal feelings of anger and resentment. However, if you are a "nice guy," then you are not supposed to feel angry, ticked off, irritated, or aggressive. Furthermore, direct expressions of anger are too risky, because the other person might be hurt and leave you, or get angry and retaliate. It is rare for someone with strong social anxiety to clearly and directly express his anger, such as looking at someone in the eye and saying, "When you did that, I felt very upset. I feel disappointed right now. I don't like that you did that."

Instead, there can be a strong tendency to avoid this level of direct confrontation. More often we simply do not say anything, and keep the uncomfortable feelings to ourselves. Or we might say, "Oh, it's no big deal. Water under the bridge," and then express our frustration in other ways, such as showing up late, breaking a commitment, or making a sarcastic joke about it. It is extremely common for people with social anxiety to have accompanying stomach and gastro-intestinal problems as well. Much of this comes from regularly suppressing anger and avoiding direct confrontation.

If we do approach the conflict, it is often after many hours or days of rumination and planning. Our feelings come out with a fair amount of explaining or self-blame. We can say things like: "Yes, I'm upset, but it's really because I'm too sensitive," or "I know it's no big deal, but I just had a hard time with it for some reason." How often do you take the blame in order to avoid a conflict?

Avoiding conflict can have a substantial negative effect on our lives. The reality is, every single relationship is going to have some sort of conflict or disagreement in it. When we try to go through life with no disagreement, without making any waves, we end up greatly limiting ourselves.

In the second part of this book, you will learn how to identify what you truly think and feel about a situation. You will also learn how to speak up for yourself, and how to develop a level of assertiveness that will greatly increase your sense of well-being in your relationships. Before you can start to do this, however, there is one final area we must discuss about the problem of social anxiety. This is your relationship with yourself—the most significant relationship you have, and one that determines the quality of all of your other relationships. If you are regularly at odds with yourself, criticizing yourself, and disliking who you are, it makes connecting with others very difficult.

The question we turn to now is: how do you treat *yourself*?

Four

REJECTING YOURSELF

Thus far you have learned that the primary cause of social anxiety is fully buying into the idea that you are not good enough. From this fundamental assumption, you talk yourself out of trying new things, avoid anything that might lead to rejection, and often do not fully speak up for yourself. Yet at the same time, you have desires and feelings. You want to go introduce yourself to that woman, you have feelings of annoyance or dislike for someone, or you internally disagree and want to challenge someone's opinion. What do you do with all of these feelings?

YOUR INNER CRITIC

The most common way that shy people deal with uncomfortable feelings is by rejecting those feelings. This comes in the form of self-judgment, and a continuous stream of internal self-criticism or self-attack. If you have been dealing with social anxiety for any length of time, then unfortunately, you know this pattern well. This inner critic can become a constant companion, criticizing and haranguing you relentlessly throughout the day.

An essential part of breaking free from shyness and anxiety is learning to deal with this inner critic in an effective and compassionate way. In the next part of this book, you will learn many powerful strategies to deal with this critic and ultimately shift your relationship with yourself. The first part of the process of becoming free from your inner critic, however, is to gain awareness of this process as it is happening. As you begin to understand why your critic is attacking you, you will automatically start to see more effective ways to respond to it.

Let's take a moment to explore just how the inner critic operates. Most importantly, we will explore why we attack ourselves, as well as the purpose of this inner voice.

THE CRITIC AT WORK

When I was an undergraduate at UC Santa Barbara, I was deathly afraid of approaching women to ask them out. I would go with several of my friends to a party with the intention of meeting women, but unfortunately this never seemed to lead anywhere.

We would cling together in a small pack, usually near the beer keg, watching women come up and refill their drinks. We would be joking with each other, laughing, and having a good time. However, whenever a beautiful woman would approach, we would fall silent, frantically trying to think of something to say. Sometimes she would look at us, awkwardly standing there in silence, while we stared down long and hard at our glasses. The twenty seconds it took to fill her glass would feel like an excruciating eternity as I realized that I was not going to say anything...again. She would leave and I would feel frustrated, ashamed, and stuck.

Even though I was silent, my mind was anything but. Inside my mind was the constant monologue of my inner critic. *You should say something! No, that sounds stupid. Oh my god, she's looking at you. You are so awkward. This is pathetic. Say something! What is wrong with you? She is way too beautiful for you. She is out of your league. Who do you think you are?*

Can you relate to this situation? What does your critic say?

More importantly, what is happening here? Why do we attack ourselves like this? What is the purpose of this critic? This will become clear as we look at more examples. For now, it is important to note that when a woman I was attracted to was nearby I would start to feel tense, nervous, and frightened. Then, my inner critic would kick into high gear.

What happens after the opportunity passes? Does your critic give a sigh of relief and take a break? I am afraid not. After a missed opportunity, my critic would unleash a new onslaught: *You are fucking pathetic! What the hell is wrong with you?! You are such a wuss. If you can't talk to a woman, then you will never be able to meet one. You will never have a girlfriend. You are a pathetic loser...*

Obviously, parties were not my scene. Perhaps I would have better luck on campus.

On one bright spring morning I attended the lab for one of my physics classes. Each person was partnered up with someone to run some tedious experiment on kinetic energy. To my surprise and delight, I was partnered up with Alexis—a stunningly beautiful woman with sandy blond hair and bright green eyes. I was love-struck immediately. The lab was a blast, although I do not think I learned much about kinetic energy. This was the opportunity I had been waiting for! As the period started to wind down, I thought about asking her for her number to see if she wanted to hang out later. Enter the critic: *There is no way she would want to go out with you. She is way too hot for you. That would be so awkward. Hitting on her will put her off. Other people in the lab will hear and think you're pathetic.*

With this voice blaring in my head on a loudspeaker, what do you think I did? At the end of the class I politely thanked her for being my partner and said I would see her in class. As I walked out of the lab and towards my next class, the same old critic showed up to let me know how bad I was: *God you're such a wuss. Why didn't you ask her for her number? That was such a perfect opportunity and you blew it. Man you're fucked up. There's no hope for you.*

Sound familiar? What is happening here? What is this strange inner voice that attacks us so relentlessly and so irrationally? First it is telling me not to try because I will surely fail, then it is attacking me for not trying! It seems like there is no way to win…

THE PURPOSE OF THE CRITIC

People who are struggling with social anxiety have some of the harshest inner critics. Once you start paying attention to this internal voice, the frequency and intensity of the self-attacks can be discouraging and disturbing at first. When I work individually with clients, they are often embarrassed to reveal what the critic is saying, and how it is saying it in their minds.

ShyQuote:
I don't want to share what he is saying. My critic is so intense and so loud. The way he is yelling at me feels so vicious. It reminds me of when I was a kid and my dad would yell at me.

Despite its criticalness and viciousness, this inner voice does have a purpose. Once you discover what that purpose is, you will be able to deal with it in an effective and transformative way. What do we know about this critic so far?

- It tells us we will fail before we try.
- It tells us we are bad after we did not try.
- It tells us we are not good enough.
- It acts up more when we are scared.

As crazy as it sounds, *this harsh voice is actually trying to protect us.*

When we are convinced that we are not good enough, and therefore not worthy of love, we feel fear and pain. Getting rejected reinforces the idea that we are unlovable, and makes us feel even worse. In response, this inner voice starts up and tells us to avoid the things that will bring on more pain, such as rejection. *The main purpose of your inner critic is to protect you from rejection.*

Remember, rejection pokes the *I'm not good enough* nerve inside of us more powerfully than anything else. If we criticize and browbeat ourselves first, we are much less likely to take the risk and face potential rejection. The inner critic is preventing you from acting in ways it deems risky. It is convinced you are unlovable and that you will certainly get rejected. It wants to keep you from hurting yourself. Unfortunately, its primary tactic is self-rejection. Often this is effective at stopping you from taking the risk, but it has the severe side effect of demolishing any feelings of happiness or self-esteem, and leaves you feeling worse and worse about yourself.

To reiterate, the sole purpose of your inner critic is to protect you and keep you in line. Its plan is for you to play small, keep your head down, and avoid drawing attention and potential rejection towards yourself. It is similar to the harsh parent that criticizes and spanks his son for running out into the street. Both operate with an attitude that says "this hurts me more than it hurts you."

At this point, you might be asking: *Wait a minute, if this inner critic is trying to stop me from taking risks, then why does it attack me so harshly after I don't take a risk? It attacks me ruthlessly when I don't approach a woman.*

After we have avoided the risk, we are left with the reality that we did not get the girl, did not get the job, and ultimately are not getting the life that we want. This is scary and painful. It also feeds into the old story that we do not have the life we want because there is something wrong with us, because we are not good enough. The critic then tries to protect us from this awful truth by whipping us into shape. This is like the parent who beats his child for failing to get good enough grades. It is the punishment mentality that so many of us grew up with. If you are not doing well enough in something, you need to be criticized and punished until you do better. Even though this is highly ineffective, many of our parents learned this from their parents. Our inner critic continues to use this approach, despite its inefficacy.

YOUR OWN WORST ENEMY

As discussed above, your inner critic wants to keep you playing small in order to stay safe and away from rejection. It comes out of the same belief that causes social anxiety, which is *I am not good enough.* The more you believe that you are not good enough, the more this voice will torment you. If you have bought into your *I'm not enough* belief by only 10%, then the voice of this inner critic has limited power over you, your feelings, and your behaviors. However, if you have fully bought into this belief, then the inner critic has 100% power and control over you. It can feel like a constant companion that follows you everywhere you go, berating you ceaselessly for your faults and inadequacies.

Sometimes, the inner critic will inform you that it is trying to make you better, trying to help you improve. While this might seem convincing on the surface, is it really true? Will the constant berating, attacks, and criticisms—the reminder that you are a "stupid pathetic loser"—*really* help you improve?

In reality, harsh criticism has the opposite effect. Research on self-compassion has shown that when people are harsh with themselves, they actually freeze up and take fewer risks in the future. They are afraid of making a mistake and experiencing that internal assault[4].

The effectiveness of using rewards and encouragement to shape behavior can be seen in all mammals. In the field of animal training, which is based on psychological principles, you can see that we are able to train animals to do amazing things. Getting a massive dolphin or orca to jump through a hoop is achieved exclusively through positive reinforcement, encouragement, and reward. You cannot beat a dolphin into performing the trick.

The worst part about this inner critic is its hypnotic quality. When we are really in our own heads, believing everything the critic says, it has a powerful ability to put us into a trance of sorts[5]. We can start to believe many things about ourselves and the people around us that are not entirely true.

---

4. For a comprehensive and incredibly thoughtful discussion on Self-Compassion research, see Kristin Neff's book, entitled *Self-Compassion* (New York: HarperCollins, 2012).

5. Tara Brach, in her seminal work on self-compassion entitled *Radical Acceptance* (New York: Bantam Dell, 2004), describes this as the *Trance of Unworthiness*.

The Closed-Loop Cycle

The inner critic's attacks not only block you from taking risks, they also actively prevent you from learning and making positive changes in your life. This occurs because the critic creates a closed-loop cycle.

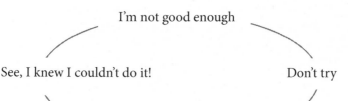

I'm not good enough

See, I knew I couldn't do it!   Don't try

Expect Failure, give up prematurely

First it tells you that you are not good enough, and therefore you will not succeed. This is often convincing enough to make you give up without trying. Why take a chance if it is not going to work out anyways? If, through some level of internal struggle, you muster up the courage to at least make an attempt, it will trip you up while you are trying. It will be in your mind, telling you that you are not doing a good enough job, or that people are bored and dislike you. Then, after you have made an attempt, it will tell you that it was not good enough and that you are a failure, *no matter what the real outcome was.*

Have you ever experienced this? Have you ever ignored the inner critic, pushed him aside, and mustered up the courage to take the risk anyway? You started the conversation with those people, gave the presentation, or went over to that woman you found compelling and introduced yourself. And best of all, it went well! She smiled and you two had a lovely conversation. What happens next?

You might have felt elated for a moment, which is perfectly reasonable and enjoyable. But sooner or later, the critic works its way back in and starts saying: *She only talked with you because she was bored. She probably doesn't really like you. Maybe there's something wrong with her. Maybe she's desperate.*

Have you ever done this to yourself—snatched defeat from the jaws of victory? All too often it is easy to explain away any success you might have experienced. As a result, even when you have a positive experience, you do not see yourself any differently. Your self-concept—the ideas you have about who you are and how desirable you are—has not changed any. The end result is the next time you are in that situation, your critic still predicts you will fail, and you have not *internalized* any of your successes. Instead of taking in this new information and saying "Wow, I guess some women actually find me attractive and enjoy when I come talk with them," the critic will find a way to discount and minimize the experience so that it does not have a positive effect on your self-image.

THE WAY OUT

As you can see, there is a momentum to the *I am not enough* belief. It is the underlying source of shyness and social anxiety. It leads you to avoid taking risks, to fear rejection, and it causes you to reject and attack yourself. It drastically reduces the quality of your life, and prevents you from approaching someone you want to meet, doing what you want to do, and just being comfortable in your own skin. Even though you might be seeing all the ways this belief is limiting your life and causing you pain, it still might be hard to let go of it. Despite seeing how much of a trap it is, it still *feels* true.

If you truly want to make a shift in your life, to free yourself from the loneliness and pain of social anxiety, then you must be willing to let go of this old belief. You do not have to know how to do this. That is what the next part of this book is all about. I have guided myself and hundreds of people through the process of letting go of this toxic belief, and I can guide you as well.

At this point, all you have to be is willing to make the shift. Hopefully you are thinking:

Yes, I want to get rid of this painful idea that I am not good enough. I am just not sure how to do it. My critic seems to have a mind of its own!

The next section will provide you with a roadmap to travel from self-doubt and self-criticism to a place of deeper confidence and belief in yourself and your inherent worth. This journey is not like flipping a light switch—you will not go from having *no confidence* to suddenly having *lots of confidence* in an instant. Confidence is something you create over time by making small choices each day. This brings you out of the thoughts in your mind and into the world around you as you begin to ask and reflect on the following fundamental questions:

- What *really* happens when I take a risk and go talk with this person?
- Is it *really* true that *everyone* will reject me?
- Is it true that I cannot handle rejection?

With an attitude of curiosity, we can start to try new things, take new actions, and ultimately get new results.

This is where the major shift starts to happen. As we begin to behave differently, we start to see that people respond differently than we feared or imagined. We start to question the idea that we are not good enough and we start to wonder if it is possible that perhaps we are worthy of love. Sometimes you might already *know* this. For instance, when you are with your dog, or when you are cuddled up on the couch with your girlfriend. The point of this program is to help you regularly know and remember your worth and value. Knowing you are valuable, worthwhile and lovable might not be something you experience all of the time, but the more often it feels true, the better your life will be.

The key to change is to gradually believe in your *I am not good enough* story less of the time. Any progress in this department leads to feeling better about yourself and leads to more opportunities in your life. If you believe you are not good enough 95% of the time, and then drop it to 80% of the time, this is a drastic improvement. If you start to believe it only 50% of the time, then the other 50% of the time you are free. Free to be yourself, and to express and share your gifts, talents, and abilities. If you buy into the negative core belief even less—dropping it to 20%, for instance—then 80% of the time you are free to be yourself.

Once you stop fully believing that you are not good enough, your life will begin to open up more rapidly than you can imagine. Once you let go of this belief, there is nothing stopping you from tapping into your purpose, your mission, and your passion in life. Without that anchor of self-doubt holding you back, you will be free to pursue the career, relationships, and partnerships that you truly desire.

That is the purpose of this program, and what we will be working on together in the second half of this book. Right now, at this moment, you do not have to know exactly how you are going to do it. You do not have to believe in yourself, or know that you have what it takes. All you have to be able to say is *it's possible.*

Is it possible that you can feel more confident? Is it possible that you can learn what you need so that you can start conversations with new people and actually enjoy the process? No matter how long you have been shy, no matter how many times you have been rejected, no matter how much fear you have experienced, it is possible for things to be different. The question for you is: would you be willing to be uncomfortable if you *knew* that doing so could radically transform your life?

If that is something that you are willing to do, then please start reading Part II to create your own map towards social freedom. If you do not feel willing, or if you are telling yourself it's hopeless because nothing will work anyway, then I suggest you take a break before reading Part II. You can put this book down for several days, weeks, or months if you like. Sit with what you have read and learned, and notice how these negative beliefs about yourself operate in your life. How do they stop you, block you, and hold you back from the life you really want? Most importantly, how do you imagine things will change? Are you hoping something will magically shift on its own? When you are thoroughly convinced that nothing will be different unless you do something different, then you are ready to read the next section of this book.

Once you have determined that you will do *whatever it takes* to break through shyness, overcome social anxiety, and live the life that you truly want, success is inevitable.

PART 2—THE SOLUTION

Five

SOCIAL CONFIDENCE

The first part of this book was designed to help you understand the major challenges and causes of social anxiety.

- It starts with a belief that there is something deeply wrong with you, and if people really got to know you they would realize you are unworthy of love and belonging.
- As a result, you need to protect yourself by avoiding people and situations where you might be judged.
- You need to avoid getting rejected, because this verifies that you are indeed unlovable.
- The more we believe this, the shyer and more anxious we feel around other people, the more we avoid rejection, and the more we reject and criticize ourselves in our own minds.

The solution to social anxiety is to let go of this limiting belief, and to truly see and know on a deep level that you are fundamentally lovable and worthwhile as you are. The rest of this book is geared towards helping you transform this belief. The program put forth in the following pages will help guide you towards letting go of this painful, limiting idea, no matter how much evidence you have, no matter how long you have believed it, and no matter how true it feels.

There may be things you want to learn, skills you want to acquire, ways you want to improve yourself. You may have an impulse to grow and expand. But for now, the goal is to see and acknowledge that you have an incredible amount to offer, and are entirely worthy of love and belonging *right now as you are.*

Achieving that goal isn't as simple as just saying "Well, that old belief doesn't serve me, so I'll pick a new one, and from now on I'll believe that I am lovable and worthwhile." If it were, there would be no need for psychologists, therapists, or coaches. People would simply make a decision and shift things on their own. The reality is that beliefs, especially the old entrenched ones, are resilient.

We developed these old beliefs when we were young, unconsciously creating them to protect ourselves. At one point in our lives, they might have even served a necessary purpose. They helped us make sense of the confusing or painful world around us. As a result, these core beliefs are embedded in our sense of self and the world around us, and take time and energy to shift.

TRUST THE PROCESS

A therapist of mine would regularly remind me during sessions to "trust the process." At first that statement annoyed me. "What the hell does that mean?" I'd ask myself. As time went on, however, I realized it meant that I did not have to completely know and understand how everything was going to work before I tried it. The point was to listen, learn, try new things, and trust that through this work I would experience the changes I was seeking.

The following chapters will guide you through a process. Together we will challenge, coerce, cajole, play, finesse and mold you from one set of beliefs and behaviors into another. This process is not binary, like flipping on a light switch. The road from shyness and social anxiety to lasting confidence in yourself is a journey, your own lifelong process of accepting who you are and becoming who you are meant to be. That is a challenge for everyone in society, not just people who are shy or anxious. It just happens to be more essential for you to figure it out in order for you to create the life you truly desire and deserve.

CREATING SOCIAL CONFIDENCE

As with any journey, it is important to know where you are headed. Knowing where you want to go gives you a sense of direction and can help you determine if you are on track as the journey progresses. One way to measure if you are letting go of your old core beliefs and adopting new ones is to pay attention to your level of social confidence.

Social confidence is a felt experience of knowing you have worth and value, being comfortable with and accepting of yourself, and enjoying connecting with other people. The following chapters will provide you with ideas, exercises, and experiments that will help you strengthen and grow your sense of social confidence. The essence of social confidence is the freedom to be yourself—to be who you really are around others. It also includes the freedom to pursue what you most value in life—whether it is a relationship, a job, or a goal.

Below you will find a list of the nine major components of social confidence. After reading each one, give yourself a number (1-10) that rates how proficient you are in this area. After you have read through the rest of this book, and completed some of the exercises, you may want to rate yourself in these areas again to see how you have grown.

Component of Social Confidence	Description	Level (1-10)
Assertiveness	Checking in with yourself to see what you are really thinking, feeling, and wanting, and then clearly communicating this. (This includes being able to ask for what you want, and to say what you do not like or do not want.)	
Self-Compassion	Your ability to treat yourself with kindness, patience, empathy, and respect, even when you make a mistake or fall short of a goal.	
Resilience	Knowing that you can handle whatever life brings you, even if it is painful or scary. You know that you will always find a way to survive and thrive.	
Inherent Worth	You know on a deep level that you are worthy of love and belonging just as you are, that you are likeable and attractive, that you have something to offer in relationships, and that people like being around you.	
Self-Efficacy	You believe you have the ability to be successful when you put effort into something. You trust in your ability to learn and figure out what you need to in order to succeed in the areas that matter most to you.	

Bold Action	Your willingness to do what scares you, to inspire and encourage yourself to take healthy risks because you know they will help you grow—even though it can be uncomfortable or scary along the way.	
Social Comfort	Your level of feeling comfortable in your own skin around other people, including people you don't know very well. This includes a general ease with who you are in social situations.	
Conversation Skills	Your level of skill at starting conversations, speaking with strangers, meeting new people, talking with groups, and otherwise being able to carry on enjoyable conversations.	
Vulnerability	You are able to share what you truly feel and think with someone else. This includes your ability to trust and to share tender feelings such as love, sadness, hurt, or joy.	

In what areas did you rate yourself highly? In which do you struggle? The most important thing to understand about social confidence is that it is not something you are just born with. This is a common myth in our culture and it leaves people feeling like they either "have it or don't."

The truth is social confidence is a skill that can be practiced, developed, and learned. Each one of the nine components is a skill or mindset that can be developed over time through practice. Whether it is assertiveness, conversation skills, or even vulnerability, you can enhance your skill in any of these areas by practicing what you learn in the following chapters.

Social confidence is like a muscle that can be strengthened over time through regular use. Much like someone who wants to become fit by going to the gym, someone who wants to become fit socially must regularly work out. Each time you take a healthy risk, speak your mind, or face potential rejection, you are building your confidence muscle.

THREE STEPS TO SOCIAL CONFIDENCE

The process of developing social confidence can be summarized in three major steps. These steps are:

1. Know Who You Are.
2. Accept Yourself. *All* of Yourself.
3. Take Bold Action.

In the chapters that follow, we will go in depth into each of these steps and provide you with a clear sense of what they are and how to use them to overcome your social anxiety. The steps work together, and do not progress in a strict, chronological fashion. For instance, you do not *fully complete* step one, then graduate to step two and so forth. Instead, you will learn and grow in these areas simultaneously, which will help you shift negative and long-standing beliefs more rapidly.

As you read, you can find ways to enhance your sense of confidence and belief in yourself by working on any of these steps. In fact, you do not even need to read them in order. You can jump to the section that will be most beneficial for you to start with right now. It is important to note, however, that it is better to review the first two steps before embarking on the third step. The third step is about taking bold action in your life, which is an essential ingredient in transforming shyness and social anxiety. However, if you start to take bold action from a place of self-criticism, self-attack, and self-hatred without yet knowing who you are, what you are about, and what you are feeling, then the road will be much more challenging.

I can state this confidently based upon my own experience. I began overcoming shyness and social anxiety by starting with step three, which is taking bold action. I learned about the process of *exposure,* which involved moving towards what scared me rather than avoiding it. Once I learned about this I said: *Well, I'm just going to expose myself to what I'm scared of until I'm not scared any more.* This can be a brilliant philosophy, but I did it with an incredible amount of perfectionism, self-criticism and self-judgment. Also, doubts lingered about who I was and what I really wanted. I had dozens of ideas about how I *should be,* and I was continually striving to live up to my unrealistic expectations.

As a result, I encourage you to review steps one and two before you jump into step three. This issue often arises when I am working with shy men in the area of meeting women and dating. They are often eager to have a shift in their lives and are impatiently waiting for the "pick-up lines." What they fail to realize is that the other steps—how they see themselves, how they treat themselves, knowing their value and purpose—all have a much greater impact on how a woman sees them.

Taking bold action, while it is an essential part of the process, is not the only step. If you take the time to *really* figure out who you are, what you want, and what your purpose is, and you do some of the exercises to increase self-acceptance, then by the time you take bold action you will be much more equipped to deal with the challenges that you will inevitably face.

DOES IT REALLY WORK?

Before embarking on this journey, many men ask me, *does this really work?*

ShyQuote

I have been shy for so long, my whole life as far as I can tell. Are a few exercises really going to do anything for me? Am I just wasting my time and energy?

Uncertainty is a perfectly normal feeling at this stage in the process. After so many years of struggle and failed attempts at change, it can be hard to believe that something could work. You might be wary of getting your hopes up, for fear that you might just be disappointed and be right back where you started. I must admit, that is possible. You might read parts of this book, try an exercise once or twice, then put it back on the shelf and never touch it again. *See, nothing works for me,* you might conclude. However, if you are determined to make a shift in your life, then this book will provide you with the exact steps you need to make that change.

How long have you been struggling with shyness and social anxiety? How long have you been on the sidelines, watching other people live their lives as you wait for a moment to engage? How many chances—for friendships, jobs, or relationships—have you passed up because of this fear?

What else has this fear cost you? How long will you continue to let this fear run your life? As you are reading these questions and thinking about the answers, you may notice a growing sense of frustration. This is a good thing. In order to make massive changes in your life—in the way you see yourself, and in the way you relate to others—you must have a strong desire to change. Nothing propels us towards growth more than a sense of frustration with our current state or situation. If you are feeling frustrated with how much you have missed out on in your life because of shyness, then now is the time to start making the shift.

In this moment you have a choice. You can decide, *right now,* that you are not going to take this anymore. That you will do *whatever it takes* to break through the ideas, fears, and obstacles that have held you back for so long. Every person with whom I have worked, who has experienced success in overcoming his or her shyness and social anxiety, began the process with this mindset. They decided they were fed up with how things were going in their lives, and they were ready to do something about it.

Take time to reflect on yourself in this moment. *Are you willing to do whatever it takes to change the way you live?* If so, then you possess a driving force deep inside you that will push you forward until you get the life you want. It will help you overcome the fears and doubts that can trip you up along the way. While this decision is necessary, it is not sufficient to trigger the change you want. Unfortunately, when the going gets tough we sometimes simply change our minds. *I don't know about doing these exercises and stuff. Life was a lot easier when I just went home and spent hours on my computer. It was more comfortable then.*

If you want to have a life that satisfies you, that feels fulfilling and exciting to you, then you must go one step further than just deciding. You must *commit* to do whatever it takes. A commitment is more permanent and unwavering than a decision. We keep our commitments, even when we sometimes don't feel like it. When committed, we will keep going, even if we get scared or uncomfortable.

I commit to doing whatever it takes to be free.

On Commitment

Until one is committed,
There is hesitancy, the chance to draw back,
Always ineffectiveness.

Concerning all acts of initiative and creation,
There is one elementary truth
The ignorance of which kills countless ideas and splendid plans:

That the moment one definitely commits oneself,
Then Providence moves too.

All sorts of things occur to help one
That would never otherwise have occurred.

A whole stream of events issues from the decision,
Raising in one's favor all manner
Of unforeseen incidents and meetings
And material assistance
Which no man could have dreamed
Would have come his way.

Whatever you can do, or dream you can, begin it.
Boldness has genius, power and magic in it.

Begin it now.

Johann Wolfgang von Goethe

Take a moment to read over the following statements, and then say each one *out loud.*

I am going to do whatever it takes.
I will not live my life like this anymore.
I commit to doing whatever it takes to be free.

It might seem silly or strange, or you might think, *Oh, I'll do that later.* The truth is the shift begins now. Saying something out loud to yourself in a room is a little strange, and it might make you a little uncomfortable. This is exactly the type of thing that will build your confidence in the long run. It involves doing something that gets you outside of your comfort zone, which strengthens your ability to act without fear of being judged by others.

Taking the risk to do something a little out of the ordinary is part of the process, and I have seen this work with hundreds of men. The only thing that can stop you is the little voice that tells you that you should not do something because it might be embarrassing or others might judge you for it.

You know what life is like under the "what will others think" tyranny. I'm asking you to take a leap and join me on the other side. I strongly encourage you to give it a shot. Say the phrases out loud and go all-out with each exercise you come across. You just might find that your entire world transforms.

Six

KNOW WHO YOU ARE

Once you get on board and are ready to begin the process of overcoming your shyness, you might be ready for action. In fact most people are hoping for a quick result that does not require too much hard work or discomfort. When it comes to meeting a woman they find attractive, they are most interested in the "pickup line." *What do I say to her that will make her want me?* The reality is social confidence does not start with what we say or do. It does not start with how we walk, our posture and body language, or how we relate to others. It does not start with anything that we can project outward. It starts from *within.*

If we do not have a clear sense of who we are and what we are doing in the world, then we do not have a *self* to be self-confident with. An essential part of overcoming anxiety and gaining confidence in yourself is deepening and strengthening your sense of self. This includes knowing who you are, what you want, what you value, what your strengths are, and what you have to offer in relationships and to the world at large.

You might be so fed up with your feelings of shyness that you want to jump into taking action immediately. If this is the case, you might be impatient with the following sections, which are designed to help you develop a strong, healthy sense of who you are in the world. You may be eager to jump ahead, figure out the "secrets," and get to the pickup lines. If so, I commend you for your enthusiasm and motivation. That will serve you well on your journey to greater confidence. If you would like, you can jump to Chapter 8, Take Bold Action, to begin creating an action plan immediately. I strongly encourage you, however, to read the following sections as you are trying new things in the world. The road to confidence is a lot more treacherous when we lack self-compassion and a strong sense of self.

Reading the sections below will help you create a deep foundation of confidence, which will go beyond "getting the girl." The ideas below will help you know yourself much better, which will allow you to not only get the girl, but *keep* the girl, and enjoy the process along the way. It will also help you be comfortable in your own skin even when you *don't* get the girl, or the job, or whatever external goal you are reaching for. The first step to knowing who you are is to know who you are *not*. To discover more, we will discuss the idea of differentiation.

DIFFERENTIATION

Are you taking too much responsibility for the way someone else feels? If someone is upset, do you automatically feel like you have done something wrong, as if you are in trouble or are somehow bad? Do you feel like you need to do something to smooth things over so they are no longer upset?

Ted was a young man who came to see me because of increased anxiety he was feeling about his relationship. He had been dating a woman for about four months, and they had been thoroughly enjoying each other's company. They would spend lots of time together and found they got along incredibly well. In spite of this, Ted sought me out for counseling.

When I asked him what he was anxious about, he said it was mostly around dealing with his girlfriend when she was in a bad mood.

"Most of the time we get along great, but sometimes when I come over to her apartment, she's upset about something. I don't really know what it is most of the time," he said as he shrugged his shoulders. "Something from work or her family or whatever. All I know is, when she is upset, I can't handle it."

"What do you mean you can't handle it?" I replied. "Does she take it out on you?"

"No, not really," he said. "She usually just wants some time alone or is quiet or something. I just start to get really anxious when she's upset. I feel like it must be something I did. I start to wrack my brain to think of what it could be that I did that is upsetting her. I try to figure out if I need to apologize or make sure that I never do whatever it is again. I feel like I'm walking on eggshells the rest of the evening."

Ted was describing a major challenge for most people in relationships, particularly people with social anxiety. Often, we quickly blame ourselves for someone else's mood, whether it is a partner, friend, coworker, or even a stranger.

WHAT IS DIFFERENTIATION?

Differentiation is a complicated word that describes a very simple concept. It essentially means "I am different from you," or "I am me, you are you." This means you are an independent person who has his own feelings, thoughts, reactions, opinions, desires, hopes, dreams, and fears. When you are with another person, you might sync up in some of these areas, but in other areas you will be completely different.

While perhaps on some spiritual or metaphysical level we are all connected, we can also make the claim that we are separated by very tangible differences and boundaries. We influence and impact each other, but we are not entirely responsible for each other's experience. This means *I have my feelings, you can have your feelings, and our feelings are not identical.* As a result, you can feel upset about something and I can feel relatively calm or unperturbed by it, or vice versa. This is natural, healthy, and to be expected in any relationship.

However, when we are shy and socially anxious, tolerating these differences can be incredibly difficult. Why would this be the case? And more importantly, how do we create a stronger sense of self that allows us to feel secure in our own thoughts, feelings, and perceptions?

WHY DIFFERENTIATION IS DIFFICULT

Do you remember the basic underlying belief that causes shyness? It is the assumption that there is something wrong with you, and that you are not enough in some way. As a result, you are not worthy of love and belonging. When you believe this idea, differentiation can be very difficult. Why?

When we believe we are unworthy, being separate and secure in ourselves can be hard because we feel like we are walking on thin ice. We feel like we are very close to harsh rejection, and that we need to compensate for our inherent inadequacy. This compensation can take many forms. For instance, we may feel the need to impress people, to be extra friendly, or to be excessively generous and giving so they will like us. The thought of disagreeing, having different opinions, or disliking something they like can feel very threatening. If they are in a bad mood, we can convince ourselves that we're the cause, and that we are somehow bad. If this is the case, then we must work hard to improve their mood so they do not see how unlovable we truly are.

When I was in my mid-twenties, I went to see a therapist for help with social anxiety. I had already learned some of the techniques I will share later in this book, and I was able to overcome my fear of approaching and asking women out on dates. My major challenge at that time was settling into a real relationship with a woman. Each time I would start to date someone, as we got closer and more intimate, my anxiety would become intolerable and I would hastily break up.

The woman I was seeing for therapy was a warm, enthusiastic Jungian analyst in her late sixties. She liked to talk about dreams, symbols, life purpose, and a number of other fascinating topics. I loved speaking with her. It was springtime in California and we would meet every Friday afternoon in her sunny upstairs office overlooking a hillside of redwood trees.

At the time, I had entered into a new dating relationship. Like many of those relationships, there was an initial period of excitement and joy, plus the satisfaction of having b*een good enough* to get the girl. I still very much needed to prove this at that time in my life. *I am good enough, see??*

Sitting in my therapist's warm office amongst towering bookshelves, I shared a challenge I was having with my new girlfriend. I told her how my girlfriend and I were spending some time in her bed and watching some shows on her laptop. I was feeling somewhat bored and antsy because I wanted to go out and do something. I didn't say that, though, because she was having a really good time watching the shows.

"Why didn't you say anything?" my counselor asked me.

"She was really enjoying being in bed with me. If I told her I wanted to do something else, she'd feel disappointed because she'd know I wasn't enjoying being in bed with her."

My counselor paused, looked at me, and made her left hand into a fist. Then she took her other hand and wrapped it around the fist. "When you are with her, you wrap yourself around her. You cease being your own self. You become a sliver of yourself and just wrap right around her. You become the skin that wraps around her and are an extension of her desires, her wants and her wishes. What does it feel like when you do that?"

That is exactly what we do when we are not differentiated. We wrap ourselves around another person and say and do whatever we think *they* want. As long as we continue to do this, we cannot know ourselves, feel confident in ourselves, or even fully enjoy ourselves around others. The key to breaking free from social anxiety is to start becoming clearer about who you are, not who you think someone else wants you to be in order to accept you.

DATING WITHOUT DIFFERENTIATION

Becoming clear of your own thoughts, feelings, perceptions, and desires allows you to differentiate yourself from another person. This is an essential component to solving social anxiety, and a necessary step in enjoying healthy, lasting relationships. In the end, dating without differentiating can make a relationship feel very confining, as if we always must be on.

I spent many years struggling with differentiation in dating. Once I learned to overcome my fear of rejection enough to start dating women, I realized getting dates was just the beginning. Once I went on several dates with a woman, I discovered I had an even deeper, more uncomfortable form of anxiety. I found I was terrified, and literally could not tolerate any negative feelings she might have. As a result, I had to protect her from feeling angry, upset, awkward, hurt, or disappointed. I had to protect her from *any* potentially negative feelings. It was so intolerable that I would do everything I could within my power to anticipate what she needed and wanted, and give it to her no matter the expense to myself, all so she would not be disappointed in me. If I thought she might want to hang out twice a week, I would suggest, unsolicited, that we hang out that often. I was going above and beyond merely saying yes to her requests, and was actually anticipating what her requests might be, then offering them as if they were my own ideas. I feared that if she asked and I hesitated, she would know that I did not really want to spend time with her, or that something else was of higher priority.

What beliefs did I have that were controlling my feelings and actions here?

1. If I don't agree with her 100% she will be hurt and disappointed.
2. If she feels hurt or disappointed, then I am a bad person.
3. If I am a bad person, then she will not want to be with me.

The entire experience was painful. When you are not differentiated, it is easy to conclude that you are responsible for someone else's feelings. If someone is upset or unhappy in any way, then you automatically conclude that you caused it or did something wrong.

- If they are angry, it means you have been disrespectful and hurt them.
- If they are disappointed or sad, it means you let them down or did not do enough.

Notice how there is no separation in these interactions, only immediate conclusions: *If you are feeling this, then I did something wrong.*

This type of relating leads to anxiety, confusion, and feelings of being trapped in your relationships. In a sense, there is not much of *you* in the relationship! There is only a facsimile or photocopy of you, just the parts of you that are nice and agreeable. While this might be what you think you have to do in order for someone to like you, it is an uncomfortable, and ultimately unsatisfying way to connect. There is a much better way that involves claiming who you are, honoring your thoughts, feelings, opinions, and desires, and sharing those clearly and directly with the people in your life.

BREAKING FREE

How do we break free from trying to be who we think we *should* be so others will like us? The first step is to take less responsibility for the feelings of the people around you. This can be an uncomfortable proposition if you have spent much of your life learning to read others and accommodate their needs and desires.

One simple, yet powerful, way to start making this shift is to regularly remind yourself with this phrase: *I am not responsible for your feelings.*

You can say this out loud when you notice yourself ruminating or replaying an interaction that made you feel guilty or uncomfortable. You can also say it in your own mind when you are listening to someone. Saying this phrase and starting to adopt this way of thinking can stir up some discomfort in people. A common response is: *Wait a minute, if I stopped taking responsibility for how others felt, I would just treat people like crap. I could say mean things or not keep my word. I would be totally self-absorbed because I'm not caring at all about what someone else feels.*

This misses the mark. True differentiation is not about being indifferent or uncompassionate. That is being detached and uncaring. Differentiation means you can still care about someone's feelings. You can even help them, support them, and listen to them. But you realize on a deep level that you are not responsible for *fixing* all of their feelings, and that you cannot *control* their feelings as much as you wish and hope you could.

Here's an example that illustrates how being differentiated can actually help you be *more* caring and responsible. Imagine that you have been dating someone for a few months and you are both enjoying each other's company. It is Friday night, and for the past few months you have spent most of your Friday nights with your new girlfriend. She would like to spend time with you tonight, but you would prefer to spend time alone or with friends. Generally, you do spend time with her, but tonight you simply do not desire that as much as doing something else.

You might feel guilty for this desire, and tell yourself: *I should hang out with her. She'll be so disappointed if I don't.* If you are not differentiated, then it will be virtually impossible to listen to and honor your own desires. You will most likely agree to hang out and make the best of it, even if part of you would prefer to be doing your own thing.

What is the cost of doing this? If you consistently deny your own feelings, needs, and desires, there will usually be consequences. As good and generous as we try to be, our true feelings find a way of expressing themselves. It might come in the form of feeling resentment, being sullen or distant and not being able to explain why, or even feeling irritated and lashing out about something insignificant. Even worse, you might be very good at hiding and suppressing these expressions of resentment. In that case, it might emerge in other ways—headaches, tension, unexplainable anxiety, or chronic stomach problems.

Regardless of how the consequences manifest themselves, it usually is impossible to hide in the long run. But there is a way to avoid these consequences—*express your true desires.* Remember, the key to beginning to differentiate is to actively remind yourself by repeating in your mind: *I am not responsible for your feelings.* Imagine speaking with your girlfriend and repeating this phrase in your mind. You can tell her that part of you wants to spend time with her, that you feel some guilt, but that you would prefer to spend the evening alone or with a friend. Let your partner have her reaction. She could feel disappointed, upset, try to convince you otherwise, or perhaps withdraw or become sullen. Regardless of the response, gently remind yourself in your mind: *I love you, but I am not responsible for your feelings.*

You might be surprised to discover that reminding yourself of this does not make you respond coldly. In truth, when you give yourself the space to have different feelings than the people around you, it allows you to empathize more with what they are feeling. You can hear her disappointment, see that she is a little sad, and respond with kindness and compassion. You are not responsible to fix her feelings or make them go away. At first this can be a scary prospect. It might seem that upsetting your girlfriend might lead her to break up with you. However, being clear and compassionate about what you want and need will actually strengthen your relationship over time.

The final step is to allow yourself to enjoy your evening alone or with a friend. Remember, when you are differentiated, it is okay for your partner to feel one way and for you to feel another. She can be disappointed, and you can have a great time reading a book or seeing a movie with your best friend.

It is important to note one final caveat about responsibility for the feelings of others. As humans, we all sometimes do things that might be inconsiderate or hurtful to others. Allowing your girlfriend or those around you to have their feelings without needing to fix them is *different* than being disrespectful or aggressive towards those around you. If you are engaging in destructive behavior, such as excessive drinking, then it is essential to acknowledge the negative impact you are having on others. In these instances, we must take responsibility for how we are treating others and make the necessary changes in our lives.

DIFFERENTIATION AND DISAPPOINTMENT

Fear of disappointing is such a common experience of social anxiety in relationships that it is worth mentioning here. When we feel anxious, it can be very uncomfortable when someone is disappointed with us. This goes back to the basic belief of shyness: *there is something wrong with me, and I am not worthy of love and belonging.*

If we believe this about ourselves, then we are also likely to feel danger when we disappoint someone. We immediately conclude that if this person is disappointed with us, it means we have done something wrong. We are bad. It is only a matter of time until they too conclude that we are no good and not worthy, and withdraw their love and affection. As a result, you might go to great lengths to avoid disappointing the people in your life, as I did for many years in relationships.

The problem with this approach, however, is that it sets an impossible standard. Disappointment is inevitable in all relationships. It is impossible for two people to have the exact same feelings and desires all of the time. Inevitably, someone will want something and the other person will not. A natural response to not getting something we want is disappointment. As long as we avoid disappointing others at any cost to ourselves, we will never truly feel safe and connected in our relationships. We will always have that nagging fear that if we were to disappoint them, they would be gone. This is a fine razor's edge to walk along.

It can be incredibly freeing and relaxing to acknowledge that you *will* disappoint people in your life, and that they will disappoint you. Disappointment does not mean the end of a relationship. Rather, it is just another emotion that is part of being a human in connection with others. It can be incredibly powerful and healing to allow yourself to disappoint someone and then realize that they still love and care about you. Repeatedly experiencing this reality can help you start to know on a deep level that you are indeed lovable and worthwhile as you are, even with your human flaws and shortcomings.

DIFFERENTIATION AND DISAGREEMENT

Creating a strong sense of social confidence comes from first having a solid, healthy, clear sense of yourself. This means being aware of your thoughts, feelings, perceptions, desires, beliefs, and opinions. The more clear you are in yourself, the more you can allow others to have their own set of thoughts, feelings, and opinions.

When we are not differentiated it can be hard to have a difference of opinions. When you are wrapped around someone and they say something, you will agree with them. If they like something, you like what they like (or pretend as if you do). If they dislike something, you dislike what they dislike. We can engage in this process both in obvious and subtle ways. Have you ever walked out of a movie with a friend, and they said, "I loved that movie?" What if you did not really like it and you thought it was boring. Do you say, "Yeah, it was great?"

One way to strengthen your sense of self is to start to pay attention to all the subtle ways you wrap yourself around another. Start to notice internally what you *really* think, feel, and believe. When you speak with someone, notice if you disagree with them on some level.

An incredibly powerful practice for developing differentiation is to actually disagree with people more. Most people with shyness and social anxiety tend to be very nice and agreeable. It can feel bad or wrong to disagree with others. In fact, for many years, I was very uncomfortable with disagreement. I just wanted to be with "positive people" who agreed with and encouraged everything I said. I believed that if you have a difference of opinion, it means you are rejecting the other person. Either I would be rejecting them or they would be rejecting me.

This is a lack of differentiation. In truth, it is impossible for two people to agree on *everything*. If you are agreeing on everything with someone, then you are either avoiding significant topics or you are wrapping yourself around the other. A key component of differentiation is the ability to disagree. If you have discomfort with disagreements, I suggest you try this Disagreement Drill.

Once a day for the next week, pay attention to when you disagree with something. When you notice this, actually say out loud the phrase *I disagree*. Depending on the setting you can say it in a playful or nonchalant way, or as part of a sentence. For example, if you are with a friend and she says "I think it's going to rain tomorrow," you could say "I disagree." Or perhaps you are at work and someone suggests an activity. If it is not fitting for you, you might say: "I disagree, I think we should try this other activity."

There is something about actually using the phrase "I disagree" that makes this exercise impactful. It succinctly expresses the very statement that we are often trying to avoid. It is direct and clear. Doing this for just a short period of time will help you develop a stronger sense of self, which allows for a greater feeling of social confidence. It will also help you see that minor disagreements are a normal part of everyday life between differentiated people.

Part of differentiation is to be able to stay with your perception and not get bowled over by someone else's opinion. It is an essential ability to be able to disagree, to be able to agree, and to be able to ask yourself, "What am I thinking here? What am I feeling, right now?" Both of these questions are very important in discovering and strengthening your social confidence. The most important question of all, however, is to ask, "What do I want?"

WHAT DO I WANT?

This is one of the most important questions you can ask yourself. Asking this question throughout the day guides you closer and closer to your inner experience, your inner truth, your innermost sense of self. It connects you with your desires, longings, wishes and hopes. It illuminates your needs in relationships, what you value in life, and what you need in order to be fulfilled.

For many of us, even feeling like we have the right to know what we want, let alone asking for it, is an unfamiliar and slightly scary prospect. The sections below will help you understand how this powerful question can help you strengthen your sense of self and improve your relationships with others.

OVER-ACCOMMODATING

Shy people (myself included) have a long, checkered history of being over-accommodating in relationships. Over-accommodation means doing what we think other people will want in order to get them to like us, and to avoid conflict.

Remember, the basic assumption of shyness is that if people saw the real me, they would reject me because there is something wrong with me. If you believe this is true, then of course you will attempt to overcome this shortcoming. As a result, you will have to be extra pleasant and nice. You have to do whatever you can to make up for this perceived deficit, which means being generous and accommodating to the people around you. This often leads to a pattern of over-accommodating: regularly doing what you *think* the other person wants, rather than doing what you want. This can happen in many ways. When you are about to go to dinner with someone, for instance, do you say, "I would love to check out that new Thai place," or do you say, "I don't care, whatever you want is fine?"

Perhaps you are flexible and actually do not care. However, it is very common for shy people to do this out of habit so often that they do not actually check with themselves to see if they have a preference.

Why don't we state our preferences? We don't state our preferences because we are afraid that when we do, another person will disagree and we might have a conflict. Or perhaps our friend, coworker, or the person we're just getting to know will secretly be disappointed and hold it against us. We might also be taking too much responsibility for everyone's experience. This is known as the "Mother Hen Syndrome." If you were to select the restaurant, you might feel responsible for everyone's experience at the restaurant. You might feel a pressure for everyone to love the food and have a great time. If they do not, that means you are not good enough, you did not pick a good enough place, and there is something wrong with you.

THE COSTS OF NOT KNOWING AND NOT SHARING

The example above is simple and somewhat trivial, but it is something we all can relate to. It also reflects how we might treat our own wants and needs on more significant topics. When we do not ask for the restaurant we want, there is a mild consequence. When we do not ask for something we truly and deeply want in a close relationship, the consequences can be more severe. When we do not ask for what we want, something happens inside of us. It can be a sense of disappointment, irritation, anger, resentment, tension, sadness, heaviness, depression or anxiety. This does not mean we are supposed to get everything we want, but not *getting* what we want is very different from not *saying* what we want.

If we want something, and it is important to us, we will experience longing, desire, hope, or yearning. If we do not share this desire with others, we must go through some process of suppressing, pushing down, or otherwise squelching this part of ourselves. This leads to the feelings mentioned above, many of which are avoidable if we merely share what it is that we truly want. There is something powerful about knowing that you can, at the very least, ask for what you want and let yourself be known. A big part of connecting with others in an authentic and satisfying way involves revealing yourself to them, including your thoughts and feelings in the moment, as well as what you do and do not want.

Sharing what you want helps other people know you, even if you do not get it. In the restaurant example above, what if the conversation went like this:

You: "I'd like to get some Thai food."

Your friend: "I don't like Thai all that much. I'd rather go to the Mexican place around the corner."

You pause, think for a moment, then say, "You know what? Let's go to the Mexican place."

While you are accommodating in a sense, this exchange feels very different than when you passively followed their lead. It is a true dialogue. And while it feels simple or small now, it will begin to impact the way you approach other, *bigger* conversations in the future, especially those related to issues you find important. This includes what you want to be doing with your time, where you would like to go for enjoyment and activities, who you would like to be with, what you would like to talk about, and what you would like to share.

It also includes very intimate and sexual desires that you might be embarrassed or ashamed to reveal: when you would like to kiss someone, how you like to kiss, when you want to have sex, what you would like to do sexually, or how often you want to have sex.

This question of "what do I want?" covers all areas of your life—from the trivial to the most significant. The deeper the desire, the more important it is to know what you truly want and to be able to express this to others.

Sharing what you want is a key aspect of social confidence. It is essential to start sharing what you want, even when you are unsure if the other person wants the same thing. Many people will wait to find out what the other person wants, then determine if they should say what they want. When we do this, we are operating from the following belief: *If they want what I want, then my want is allowed. If they do not, then my want is wrong or selfish, and I must hide it.*

The key is to be able to put yourself out there by revealing what you want. This can leave you feeling vulnerable, especially when the desire is deep or personal. *This is partly why we often do not fully acknowledge what we truly want—to others or to ourselves.*

WHAT STOPS US?

There are several blocks we must overcome before we discover and learn how to share what we truly want. When I work on this skill with clients who have spent much of their lives accommodating others, they are surprised to realize that they do not really know what they want. In fact, even just asking themselves what they want can bring up some resistance.

A while back I met a young woman named Jennifer. She was a beautiful, intelligent, and highly empathic person. She performed well in school and was also a skilled athlete. Despite all of these strengths, she had bought completely into the idea that she was not good enough and not worthy of love. As a result, she had crippling social anxiety that prevented her from creating the friendships and romantic relationships she wanted in her life. As we began to explore what she truly wanted, she started to see the ideas that stopped her from discovering her real desires. The following conversation involves her spending time with her mother.

Jennifer: So my mom wanted me to go over to her house for dinner, but that was the same night Kelly said she was free. I had already told Kelly I would hang out with her, so now I'm stuck. I don't know what to do.

Aziz: What do you want to do?

Jennifer: Well my mom makes these elaborate meals that she spends all day preparing and it would be really nice to be there with her, but Kelly said the other day that she feels like we don't see each other that much any more.

Aziz: I can hear what your mom wants and what Kelly wants, but where is Jennifer in this situation? What does she want?

Jennifer: I don't want to disappoint either of them!

Aziz: Hmm, that puts you in a bind. It seems like no matter what you do, one of them might feel some disappointment.

Jennifer: (nods)

Aziz: But I still haven't heard what you truly want. If you could take your pick and do whatever you liked, without any consequences, what would you do?

Jennifer: I'd want to stop by mom's for a bit, have a quick bite, then meet Kelly for a drink afterwards. But that's terrible. My mom will have spent all day working on this meal and I just swing by, eat, and leave.

Aziz: Wanting to do that is "terrible?"

Jennifer: Yeah, it's selfish.

As you can see in this conversation, Jennifer had resistance to even discovering and sharing what she wanted, because she labeled it as "selfish" and "terrible".

SOCIAL ANXIETY AND SELFISHNESS

Many people who struggle with shyness and social anxiety have a very strong set of values related to kindness, giving, and being supportive of others in their lives. This is a noble way to live, and will often greatly benefit you in your relationships.

However, it is also very common for people with social anxiety to have a strong fear of being seen as *selfish*. They believe that when they look at and prioritize what they want, they're putting themselves first, which is selfish and wrong. Indeed many of us have gotten the message that it is "good to share" and that "giving is better than receiving." These concepts are part of the socialization process that helps us live cooperatively with other people. The problem is we can take these messages too far and end up being self-denying[6].

---

6. Richard and Rachael Heller thoroughly describe what self-denying is in their book *Healthy Selfishness* (Des Moines: Meredith Books, 2006).

Self-denying occurs when you put the needs, desires, and preferences of others above your own. Instead of realizing that both your needs and their needs matter, you assume that their needs matter more, and yours are secondary. Any time you think about putting yourself first or taking care of your needs, you get the feeling that you are selfish, bad, or wrong.

You might believe that asking for what you want is selfish. Is this really true? Is it reasonable to expect yourself to go through life always taking care of others and squelching, denying, and suppressing your own desires? Not only does this lead to more feelings of anxiety and depression, it can also damage your relationships. Contrary to what we might have been taught, continually sacrificing yourself for another does not create lasting, healthy connections between people. It creates feelings of resentment, low self-esteem, and anxiety, and can cause you to feel overwhelmed. We fear that if we ask for what we want, we will appear selfish and people will dislike us. However, asking for what you want actually produces the opposite effect. When you speak clearly about what you would like, people get a much better sense of who you are. Even better, you actually have a much higher chance of receiving what you want when you request it!

The Fear of Rejection

When we are operating from the belief of shyness—that there is something wrong with us and that we don't deserve love and belonging—then we naturally assume people will reject us. We assume those around us will immediately reject our wants and desires. If you want to spend time with someone, you will assume that they probably would not want to spend time with you. If you want to sleep with someone, you might automatically conclude that there is no way they would want to sleep with you. With this assumption of rejection, it is easy to conclude that people will find all of our wants and needs to be annoying, weird, or off-putting.

ShyQuote:
I imagine that if a woman knows that I am interested in her sexually, then she will immediately be turned off, freaked out, and annoyed.

In short, the more you are buying into the fundamental belief of social anxiety, the more you will assume that you, and whatever you want, will be rejected. As a result, you might avoid asking for what you want, or you may wait until you know that it is absolutely safe to ask for what you want because the other person wants it as well.

As you will see later in this book, it is absolutely essential that you challenge the assumption that people will reject you, and be put-off by your wants or requests. One basic way to begin challenging that assumption is to experiment by actually asking for something and seeing what happens. You will learn more about how to do this in Chapter 8, which covers taking new actions in the world.

THE TRUTH ABOUT YOU AND WHAT YOU WANT

Rather than being imposing, annoying, or unattractive, knowing what you want and asking for it is actually very compelling for the people in your life. It allows them to know you and to fully see what is going on in your mind and heart. This is what true connection and intimacy are all about—sharing what you are thinking and feeling in the moment. Friendships and relationships are not based on you hiding your own wants and doing whatever you think the other person needs.

In fact, if you continually give without acknowledging and sharing your own desires or needs, an imbalance starts to develop. Some people tend to feel uncomfortable with receiving and not being able to give back. Others will not respect you as much and may take advantage of your generosity. This leads to the feeling that you are being taken for granted, or that you are being "walked on."

In order to ask for what you want, you must give yourself full permission to explore this question on a daily basis:

"What do I want in this situation?"

This exploration is not selfish. Rather, it is an exploration into taking care of yourself. You are discovering how to operate with a healthy level of self-interest. You are curious about who you are, what you want, and what you are feeling. This comes from a place of honoring and valuing whatever it is you are experiencing.

As you ask for what you want more frequently, you might start to realize that people do not always reject your requests. Even if someone does not want what you want, as a differentiated person you can say, "Hmm, he doesn't want that. That's OK. I still want that." If someone does not want the same thing as you, does that mean that what you wanted was wrong? We can have so much shame and judgment around our personal, vulnerable desires, and especially our deeper desires:

- I want this person to pay attention to me.
- I want this person to love me.
- I want to have someone listen to me while I share about my day.
- I want to try a certain sexual position.
- I want to ask this person to stop doing something that annoys me.

It can be very uncomfortable to reveal our desires—and ourselves—in this way. Yet every time we avoid doing so, we allow the belief that there is something wrong with us to continue. Every time you *do* ask for a want, even if it is declined, you are strengthening something inside of yourself. You can experience a *no* and see that you survive, and that there is nothing wrong with what you wanted. You also get closer to the core of who you are, and gain more trust in yourself. Each time you discover what you want and speak it, you are honoring who you are in this moment. The more you do this, the stronger your sense of self will become, which will help you handle rejection and disappointment. You will be able to feel more comfortable in who you are and what you like, do not like, and what you desire.

Beyond strengthening your sense of self, beyond knowing yourself better and feeling more comfortable with your own desires, there is one major benefit to asking for what you want. That is, what if it actually turns out well and you get more of what you want? What if you ask someone to help you move and they willingly help you? What if you ask someone to stop interrupting you and he does? What if you want to kiss someone and they want to kiss you back? What if you start getting more of what you want in life, simply by having the courage to ask for it?

Know Your Value

Getting a clearer sense of who you are and what you have to offer the world is a primary step in overcoming social anxiety. This gives you a solid perception of yourself that allows you to relate to others in a more empowered way.

Thus far you have been learning how to take less responsibility for the feelings of those around you, how to discover what you truly want, and how to start asking for it. The latter can be quite challenging, especially if doing so makes you feel anxious or uncomfortable. Do not worry, you will learn much more about how to systematically approach what scares you in Chapter 8. For now, it is essential to keep exploring who you are, since this is the foundation of social confidence.

The next step of knowing who you are will require you to accurately perceive yourself, especially your strengths, abilities, and positive attributes. The more you acknowledge these parts of yourself, the easier it will be to feel confident.

THE NEGATIVE FILTER

Most people I work with who have social anxiety perceive themselves and the world around them through a particular filter. This phenomenon is not unique to this group—all of us filter the world through our own expectations, beliefs, histories, perceptions, and experiences. However, the filter for social anxiety is fairly unique and often has a consistent pattern.

People with social anxiety often filter out strengths: the things that make you capable, strong, resourceful and competent. These are often ignored, explained away, or in some other way determined not to count. In addition, the filter lets in a whole host of your flaws, shortcomings, weaknesses and anything else that makes you inferior to others.

Here is a brief excerpt from a session I did with a client who was operating with this filter. As you read our conversation, see if you can determine how he sees himself:

Karl: The other day I was at work and several of my coworkers were hanging out in the break room. Usually I just walk in, get my snack and get out of there as fast as I can, but recently I've been practicing hanging out there more.

Aziz: Good!

Karl: Yeah, but I have no idea how to actually engage beyond small talk. It sounds like they do some fun stuff outside of work, going to parties and music shows and stuff, but I have no idea how to join them.

Aziz: What happens when you talk with them about what they did the weekend before, or about shows they've seen recently?

Karl: I don't really talk or ask anyone directly. I am more on the outside, listening in on the conversations.

Aziz: Do you want to be more involved?

Karl: Yes! I just don't know how.

Aziz: What if you asked one of them directly?

Karl: I can't do that. It would be so awkward. I'm that weird guy who hangs around the break room now, eavesdropping on conversations. There is no way they would invite me to anything.

Aziz: That's a pretty harsh appraisal of yourself. It sounds like you don't think you have much to offer.

Karl: Not really. I don't know anything about the music they're into, I don't do anything exciting, and I'm boring to talk to.

Aziz: You sound like a prosecutor making a case. A very compelling case as to why you have nothing to offer.

Karl: It's just the uncomfortable truth.

Aziz: I think I have a clear sense of your shortcomings, but what are your strengths? What is good about you? What do others get from being around you?

Karl: *[long pause]* I don't know.

Aziz: What if you were to take a guess?

Karl: I've been told I'm a good listener. And I can make good pasta.

Aziz: Great, what else?

Karl: I don't know. I'm only a good listener because I'm too polite to interrupt people. I'm often thinking about other things. And my pasta is good, but it's pretty unhealthy. That's all I can think about, is how the two things I mentioned aren't true.

Aziz: It's amazing how our minds do that, isn't it? It looks like the prosecutor is still going and is cross-examining anything positive you say about yourself.

◦◦◦◦◦◦

Do you relate to anything Karl said? Did you notice how Karl was easily able to access his shortcomings and flaws, but had a much more difficult time identifying and acknowledging his strengths and his value? There is a reason why Karl, and most people with shyness and social anxiety, undervalue themselves. It is the result of a skewed *self-concept.*

YOUR SELF-CONCEPT

Your self-concept is a term used in psychology to describe how you see yourself. Are you tall or short? Fat or skinny? Attractive or unattractive? Smart or dumb? There are thousands of adjectives we can use to describe ourselves, and our self-concept is a collection of these descriptors.

If I were to ask you to tell me about yourself, your response is your self-concept, or how you perceive yourself in that moment. Our self-concepts are very subjective, based on comparison to others, and often change depending on how we are feeling. Some parts of our self-concept are fairly objective and accurate, such as: *I am 5 ft. 9 inches tall, I have brown hair, I live in Portland.*

Other parts of our self-concept are very subjective and often based on observations we made a long time ago. For example, someone's perception of herself may include: *I am not funny.* This is part of her self-concept. If someone asked her, "Are you funny?" she would say, "No, I am not."

Not funny to whom? Everyone? All the time? Are you ever funny? Do you amuse yourself sometimes? Has *anyone* ever laughed at anything you have said? When we start to ask specific questions, these parts of our self-concept usually do not hold up. We start to see that they are *generalizations* we have made about who we are. For those with social anxiety, their self-concept is often filled with such generalizations, whether or not the concept is completely accurate.

In the example above, we discovered that, according to Karl's self-concept, he was boring and unexciting. Did you notice how strongly he believed these things? It was as if he were asserting he had brown hair, or that he wore a size nine shoe. A key step in overcoming social anxiety is changing your self-concept. More specifically, it involves challenging your strongly held negative perceptions of yourself while also searching for more realistic perceptions of your strengths and abilities.

As you have been reading this, what have you discovered about your own self-concept? Do you tend to see yourself in a negative light? Do you use generalizations like Karl?

Here are some common negative phrases that people with social anxiety use as self-descriptions:

- I'm boring.
- I'm awkward.
- I'm unattractive.
- I'm ignorant, immature, or inexperienced.

On the flip side, when asked about their strengths, people often struggle to identify them or discount their importance.

BLOCKS TO ACKNOWLEDGING YOUR STRENGTHS

As soon as you ask the question: "What are my strengths?" you might experience a feeling of discomfort, resistance, or anxiety. Or perhaps you come up with a possible answer, such as, "I am kind and compassionate," but your mind immediately jumps in with: *No you're not. If you are so kind and compassionate, how come you didn't listen to your friend the other day? You aren't kind all the time.*

Why is it so hard to identify, acknowledge, and own our strengths? What stops us from fully knowing what we have to offer others, and acknowledging our value?

The primary block to acknowledging our strengths comes down to two major fears:

1. I will be seen as egotistical and full of myself.
2. I don't want to say I'm better than anyone else.

If you are holding one or both of these concerns, then it will be very difficult to fully identify with your strengths. These are compelling reasons *not* to feel good about what you have to offer. Let us take a moment to look at each one in turn to help you realize that owning your value is actually an incredibly altruistic and egalitarian thing to do.

You egotistical bastard...

Almost all people with social anxiety fear that others will see them as egotistical, self-centered, selfish, self-focused, or arrogant. Such traits are not exactly revered in our society, and people with shyness are especially averse to being seen in this light. Many shy people will go to great lengths to avoid ever being accused of such vile behaviors. Why is this?

As you recall, the underlying belief of shyness is *I am not good enough and not worthy of love.* The main way to overcome this belief is to work extra hard to be likeable, to be good, to be worthwhile. Part of that extra work is to avoid doing anything that might turn people off, including being self-focused and unaccommodating to the requests of others. While the urge to be cooperative, inclusive, and altruistic is incredibly healthy and often leads to deep bonds of connection, it can be taken too far. People with social anxiety have such a heightened awareness of being seen as selfish or egotistical that they go to the opposite extreme. In their minds, they are required to be the epitome of selflessness, *all of the time.*

ShyQuote:
As I started to pay attention to it, I realized that everywhere I went I was expecting myself to be kind, attentive, and giving to everyone. I was supposed to like everybody. I feel like I'm supposed to be like Gandhi or Mother Teresa or something.

What does this have to do with having a healthy self-concept, seeing your strengths, and appreciating your value? Somewhere along the way, many of us have learned that acknowledging we are good at something means we are being egotistical or arrogant. We automatically label any sort of claim of competence in ourselves or others as "bragging."

This perception does a great disservice to you and to those around you. If you truly want to break free of a lingering feeling of anxiety and fear around others, you must learn to change how you see yourself and your strengths. In truth, acknowledging and owning your strengths actually makes you *less* egotistical. When someone brags a lot, talks incessantly about who or how much they know, or otherwise makes a big deal about their abilities, they are usually overcompensating for an underlying feeling of insecurity or inadequacy. This comes from not really acknowledging and owning their strengths.

Imagine two people who are studying the martial art of karate. One is early in the process and has acquired a mid-level belt. The other is a seasoned high-degree black belt who has been training for several decades. If you were to have a conversation with these two people, which one do you think would be more likely to tell you all about the latest moves he or she can pull off?

Most likely, it would be the newer student. He would be excited and proud of his accomplishments and eager to tell you all about how much he can do and how much he knows. What about the seasoned veteran who has been doing this for twenty years? Would he eagerly tell you how good he is, how much he knows? Most importantly, which one knows on a deep level that they have mastered the art of karate? Which one *knows* their strength and *owns* their value?

When we fully acknowledge and own our own strengths, we simply know on a deep level what we are good at. We can draw a sense of self, pride, identity, and worth from these qualities. The more we truly own these strengths, the less we need to brag, explain, or otherwise try to impress others. We simply *know* our value.

On the other hand, when we refuse to acknowledge these positive qualities in ourselves, we actually become *more* egotistical. While it might appear that we are being humble and avoiding arrogance, in reality we do not feel good about ourselves. Without knowing our value, we consistently feel insecure and inadequate. When someone else demonstrates one of their strengths, we might feel inferior and envious. As much as we try to suppress these feelings, they will usually emerge in biting comments or internal self-attack. However, when you are fully rooted in knowing what makes you valuable, in what you have to offer, then someone else demonstrating their strength is no longer threatening. It allows you to see and appreciate them at a greater level than you ever could when you were disconnected from your own strengths.

Superiority avoidance

The second major block to acknowledging our strengths is the fear of claiming to be better than others. Having felt inferior for so many years, we can gain a finely tuned ability to perceive status and social hierarchy. If you have been shy for a long time, you may have perceived yourself as being at the bottom of this hierarchy. You know how bad it feels to believe that you are inadequate or inferior. As a result, you might be very concerned about other people feeling the pain of being inadequate.

This points to another *positive* quality of people with shyness: they are often very socially perceptive and aware of how others feel. They tend to be considerate and concerned about the welfare of others. This makes them highly skilled in helping professions such as nursing, counseling, or teaching.

However, like altruism and cooperation, consideration can be taken too far. In an attempt to protect others from feelings of inferiority, many people with social anxiety will never acknowledge their strengths. This strategy, while well intentioned, actually does not help either person in the situation. It is based on the assumption that there is a limited amount of value to go around, and that if you are good at something, someone else is automatically less valuable. It is also based heavily on our tendency to assume others feel and think the same way we do. If we often feel inferior when we hear about someone else's strengths, we assume that *everyone* feels inferior when they hear about someone else's strengths.

In reality, once you start to acknowledge and own your strengths, you will stop responding to other people's strengths with feelings of inferiority and inadequacy. Before you know your own strengths, your mind might do something like this: *Oh, he's really good at running. I'm not that good at any sport. In fact, I'm not that good at anything.*

Once you know what you are good at, and are able to completely own it, your thought process might be more like this: *Wow, he's really good at running. That is amazing that he can do that much with his body. I want to learn more about that. I wonder if I could get some tips on how to run more myself without getting injured.* In this scenario, there is no comparison of your inherent worth as human beings. You are simply acknowledging that this person is highly skilled at running, and that you would like to be better at running.

What about the realization that not only is he better at running, but he is better at running than you are at any sport, or at *anything?* How do you not feel "less than" around that? The answer comes once you are fully aware of the many strengths and valuable things you offer the world. In fact, comparing yourself less to others is just one of the many benefits of discovering and acknowledging your strengths.

BENEFITS OF KNOWING YOUR STRENGTHS

Once you know what you are good at, what you enjoy, and what makes you thrive, you will be able to shift your self-concept from being overly negative to being more positive and realistic. You will be able to see yourself and others more clearly. As you have been reading about strengths, you might already be forming some ideas about what your strengths might be. If so, great! Just let your mind explore what these qualities might be. In the next section we will go through a process that will help you clearly identify and start to internalize these strengths.

Before we do that, however, it is helpful to see what the benefits are of discovering your value. There are three major benefits to knowing your strengths:

1. Stronger sense of self.
2. Greater self-acceptance.
3. Fewer comparisons.

Below we will briefly discuss each of these benefits, before we move on to identifying and owning your strengths.

A strong sense of self

When you are aware of your strengths, you have access to a greater sense of pride, ability, and accomplishment. You have a clear sense of what makes you valuable, and what you bring to others and to the world. In short, you *matter*. When we are disconnected from this, we have a weaker sense of ourselves, and we often conclude that we do not matter. Our thoughts, feelings, perceptions, and opinions are not as important as the next person's.

A strong sense of self allows you to interact with others in a less inhibited, less bashful way. You have nothing to apologize for because you are worth just as much as anyone else on the planet. If someone disagrees with you, does not like you, or rejects an offer you make, you are able to take it in stride. You realize that not everyone is going to like you, and that not everyone is going to see your strengths. And that is okay because *you* know on a deep level that you have a lot to offer and there are many people out there who will see and appreciate that.

Greater self-acceptance

Self-Acceptance is such an important part of the solution to social anxiety that it has an entire chapter in this book dedicated to it. When you are able to accept yourself for who you are in this moment, a deep sense of peace and relief can begin to emerge. Knowing your strengths allows you to more clearly acknowledge and accept your weaknesses. Your flaws, shortcomings, setbacks, and failures are no longer evidence of personal inadequacy, but are merely part of being a human being.

Your knowledge of your strengths serves as an anchor to keep you grounded in the face of setbacks or mistakes. *Yes, I might need to work on this area, or I might be struggling here, but I know that I am also an incredibly bright, capable, clever person who can figure things out.* Knowing your strengths keeps you balanced and prevents you from coming to negative and generalized conclusions, such as *I'm a bad person*, or *I'm boring*. It allows you to see that you are a complete person with moments of strength and glory, as well as moments of confusion and falling short.

Fewer comparisons

One of the major benefits of owning your strengths is that you start to compare yourself less to other people. Most of the comparisons we make are negative and generally have us on the weaker end. *He's stronger than I am. She's smarter than I am. He's better looking than I am. He's funnier and more outgoing than I am...*

These comparisons carry a heavy weight, as we are often subconsciously concluding that because this person is *funnier* than we are, he is a *better human being*. Next to him, we do not deserve to exist. This type of extreme comparison is born out of discounting your own strengths and value to the world. Once you are able to claim your strengths and internalize them, comparisons take on a very different quality. The human worth element is taken out of the equation and the charge is removed. You are able to simply acknowledge if someone is taller, smarter, faster, better or worse looking. There is no conclusion about their worth as a person.

This comes out of the realization that everyone has things they are good at—strengths, abilities, personality traits, etc.—as well as things in which they are lacking. Do not be fooled—that attractive, witty, outgoing person has challenges, flaws, and insecurities just like you do. *Everyone* does.

WHAT ARE YOUR STRENGTHS?

As you have been reading the above sections, you may have noticed passing thoughts about what some of your strengths could be. If you pay attention to them now, what do you notice? Do you have clear ideas about what your strengths are, or are they faint glimmers of possibility? When you put down the fear of being egotistical or superior, and simply examine what you are good at, what comes to mind?

Take a moment to be over the top, just between you and the words on this page. No one else will know. If you were going to be full of yourself for a moment, what could you admire about yourself? Imagine there are several people who are raving fans of yours. They are excitedly waiting to see you, perhaps to have you autograph something for them. As they eagerly anticipate seeing you, they are chatting about how amazing they find you, and what they specifically like about you. What would they say?

Oh my god, I can't wait to see Aziz! He is so talented! He's intelligent, incredibly driven, and is always learning new things. He is an excellent communicator, he is really patient with others, and a really compassionate guy. I bet he is an amazing dad!

What would they say about you?

If you are rolling your eyes at this exercise and noticing resistance to identifying your strengths, I encourage you to go back to the sections a few pages ago that discuss the blocks to, and benefits of, acknowledging your strengths. See if you can let go of whatever is stopping you from really connecting to what makes you special, unique, and admirable.

Seeing greatness outside of you

Another great way to tap into your strengths is to do the following thought experiment. Imagine someone you really admire. Someone you find absolutely incredible. It could be someone you know personally, someone in your family, a friend, someone you've seen in movies, a politician, an artist, author...anyone from any time period. Call that person to mind now, and notice what *specifically* you admire about them. Do you love their intelligence? Their ability to impact others? Their strength or physical prowess? Their compassion and kindness? Think of at least three traits or abilities you admire in this person. If you like, you can take a moment to write them down on a sheet of paper. Do not continue reading until you have come up with three specific traits.

Why does this person stand out to you? Out of all the amazing people who are living and who have lived, why did you pick *this* person? These abilities?

The truth is, we admire the people we resonate with most. The traits you identified are either traits you yourself have, but are not acknowledging, or traits you have not yet fully developed. For example, if you admire someone because she is an amazing author and storyteller, then you might already be a very good writer or storyteller, and you are just not acknowledging it. It can be threatening to acknowledge our greatness, abilities, and power. It is much easier to project it onto someone else. *That* person is amazing, *they* have those abilities. At this point, you might be saying: *well, that sounds nice, but the reality is I haven't written anything since grade school!* In that case, the reason you find this author so inspiring is because you have that very same ability lying dormant inside of you. If you did not, why would you care about this person's abilities?

Take a moment to look at the list of traits and abilities you listed for the person you admire. Can you see how you might already be demonstrating those same abilities? Can you see how some of them might be dormant or not fully developed inside of you?

Picking your strengths

Do you have a list of five abilities, attributes, traits, or skills that are your strengths? Take a moment to write out a list of possible candidates. Perhaps your list will be longer than five and you can mark off the ones that you do not fully see as personal strengths.

If you are struggling to imagine anything you are good at, you can explore the list of possible strengths below and draw some ideas about your own abilities. Mark the strengths you think relate to you:

Strengths		
• Intelligent	• Determined	• Good Singer
• Witty	• Decisive	• Good Musician
• Funny	• Curious	• Good Artist
• Playful	• Love of Learning	• Good Athlete
• Kind	• Non-judgmental	• Courageous
• Compassionate	• Empathic	• Honest
• Patient	• Good Listener	• Loyal
• Loving	• Physically Attractive	• Humble
• Generous	• Creative	• Self-Control
• Grateful	• Optimistic	• Passionate

Which ones from this list stand out? Can you identify several of these abilities as things you possess? Create a list of your top five strengths on a sheet of paper now.

Own them

As you look at your list of strengths, what is your experience? Do you agree with the list? Do you believe that you have these qualities and that other people could be attracted to you because of these qualities?

ShyQuote:

What are my strengths? I'm a pretty bright guy I guess... and I'm a kind person?

When one of my clients said this to me, his voice increased two octaves as he said the last few words, indicating a huge question mark. Am I really a kind person? Can I actually say my strengths out loud?

While identifying what makes you special, admirable, and attractive to others is an important part of the solution to social anxiety, it alone is not likely to shift how you feel about yourself. It is one thing to *identify* your strengths, and something entirely different to *own* them. Owning our strengths involves knowing them on a deep level, trusting in them, and believing that we do in fact have some pretty amazing qualities. It involves carrying this knowledge with dignity and self-respect, instead of doubt and pre-emptive apology.

The general attitude of owning your strengths can be summed up in two words: *Of course.*

- Of course I am intelligent.
- Of course I am funny.
- Of course I am an attractive guy.
- Of course I am kind and patient.
- *Of course.*

So how do we get there? How do we take these newfound strengths that we are still secretly doubting and start to fully own them?

Emphatic declaration

"Any idea, plan, or purpose may be placed in the mind through repetition of thought."

~ *Napoleon Hill*

What we say to ourselves on a daily basis, on an hourly basis, on a moment-to-moment basis, has a powerful effect on how we see ourselves. We are constantly altering and adjusting how we see ourselves. This is also known as our identity. Most of us who have difficulty acknowledging our strengths tend to have a negative identity. We tend to repeat certain things to ourselves dozens of times per day, if not more. Things such as:

● That was stupid.
● People will think I'm incompetent.
● No one would hire me.
● I'm a loser.
● I'm pathetic.
● I'm no good at this.

While most of the time we are not saying these phrases out loud, they do sometimes slip out in our conversations or when we have made a particularly obvious blunder. You may have even had the experience of making a mistake, then exclaiming "Idiot!" out loud.

The process of emphatic declaration takes the same principle and turns it to your advantage. Through repetition, you can start to alter the way you see yourself, thus changing your identity. The process is simple, yet powerful. It involves taking your list and stating your strengths out loud, using a full, strong tone with slightly louder volume than you would normally use in regular conversation. You firmly assert the strength in a way that links it to your identity. The most powerful and efficient way to do this is to use the phrase, "I am." For example:

- I am intelligent.
- I am funny.
- I am witty.
- I am creative.
- I am loving.

Say each phrase out loud, with emphasis, energy, and emotional intensity. Keep in mind that you may have repeated negative statements about your weaknesses thousands of times over the years. In order to create momentum for your mind to start focusing more on your strengths, it requires emotional intensity and frequent repetition. You can do this exercise while driving, brushing your teeth, and many other times throughout the day. You can even do it silently in your mind while in line at a store. When you are alone and comfortable, it is essential to say these things *out loud*. Doing so causes your mind to speak the phrases and hear them, which creates more of an impact on your subconscious.

If you would like to increase the effect, you can go on a small rant after you have stated your strength. This involves saying whatever comes to mind that supports the statement you just made. For example:

I AM creative! I generate lots of ideas and I actually turn them into cool projects that I complete. I am always thinking of new things to do and how to put them together in new ways.

I AM loving. I treat the people in my life so well. I am warm and affectionate with my friends, my family, my girlfriend, and my cats. People around me can feel my warmth and love.

What is important here is not the specific language you use, but rather the energy and intensity with which you say it. This technique is a powerful part of your process of being free from social anxiety. By itself, it may not be sufficient to dramatically change your identity. That requires finding new evidence and applying all of the other skills you are learning in this book. However, it is an essential component that can help you on your path to greater freedom, choice, and confidence.

Seeking evidence

In Part I you discovered how we have the tendency to seek confirmation for what we believe. We tend to find what we are looking for. Do you remember that exercise of looking around the room and finding everything red you could see? Finding evidence for our weaknesses and shortcomings works the same way. Most people with social anxiety have a tendency to find evidence as to why they are inadequate, inferior, unattractive, and so on. Meanwhile, they ignore any evidence that suggests they might have positive, admirable qualities.

To shift this pattern, it is essential to start looking for evidence of your strengths. Through writing your strengths down and practicing emphatic declaration, you are guiding your mind to pay more attention to these qualities in yourself. During your day, actively search for evidence of how you demonstrate or act out one of your strengths. In your journal, record how you used at least one of your strengths. It does not have to be a grand or dramatic demonstration, just a simple acknowledgement of something small you did that shows you do in fact have this quality. For example:

Strength: Compassion
Evidence: Today at work when Judy was frazzled and having a hard time, I went over to her after the meeting and asked her how she was doing. She shared news about her kids and some of her fears about work. I listened attentively and did not judge her. I am compassionate.

Notice how the evidence ended with a declaration of the strength with the words "I am." Remember, when it comes to determining our identity (how we see ourselves), nothing is more powerful than the words "I am."

THE POWER OF PURPOSE

"True happiness is not attained through self-gratification, but through fidelity to a worthy purpose."
~ *Helen Keller*

An essential part of knowing yourself includes knowing why you are here, or at least having a good guess as to why you are here. After all, no one knows objectively what the purpose of life is, but each of us has the ability to create our own purpose and meaning for our lives.

Meaning and purpose are incredibly important personal questions we all have to grapple with to make sense of why we are here, what we are doing, and what life is all about.

This might sound like a deep, philosophical question, and your eyes might start to glaze over. *The purpose of my life? What does this have to do with social anxiety? What does this have to do with me being able to have a girlfriend, or get the job that I want, or speak up to my boss?*

Those are good questions, and our exploration about the purpose of your life is not going to be an abstract, philosophical discussion. I promise you this question can produce answers that will profoundly affect your day-to-day life. In addition, the answers you come up with will help give you the strength and courage to take the risks necessary to get the things you truly desire in this life.

You can think of your purpose as consisting of two levels. First, there is our day-to-day purpose—the outcomes we strive for, and focus we bring to any activity. Then, there is our larger life direction—our life purpose. This is a deeper exploration of who you are in the world, who you want to be, and what you stand for. Being aware of this will give you a deep sense of pride in who you are, and will help you weather the inevitable storms of life.

Your day-to-day purpose

Have you ever had the strange experience of being in a room in your house, and not knowing why you went in there in the first place? You have a clear memory of deciding to go to this room, knowing that there was something you were supposed to do in there. But now that you are there, you cannot for the life of you remember what that thing was?

It is a frustrating experience. It also highlights the power of purpose in every moment of our lives. In each activity, whether it is going to the supermarket, going into a certain room of our house, or starting a conversation with someone, we have a reason for doing it. We have an outcome that we desire. In other words, we have some purpose. The clearer our purpose, the more likely we are to work towards achieving it. Have you ever been to the supermarket when you are hungry? Perhaps you entered with the vague purpose of: *I'm going to the store to get some food.* What happens then? For most of us, our quick trip to the store can turn into a forty-minute endeavor of aimlessly searching through the aisles, grabbing random items that seem good in the moment. We get back home, unload our bags and ask ourselves, "What the hell did I buy? I still have nothing for lunch this week."

In contrast, have you ever been to the store when you had an exact list of the items you wanted to purchase? How was your experience in the store? Most likely, you efficiently walked the aisles, grabbed the items you knew you needed, paid for them, then left.

Let's apply this to the realm of your social life. When you talk with someone, do you have a purpose? Yes, you absolutely do. You might not be aware of it, but you will always have a purpose to your interaction. This purpose is going to have an impact on how you relate to the person and how you feel during the interaction.

For example, imagine you are at work and want to speak with your coworker, Ted. During a break you decide to go over and start a conversation. When you talk with Ted, what is your purpose? What is your desired outcome? Why do you want to do this? What do you want? Being able to identify, understand, and answer these questions is incredibly important, as the answers will determine how you are going to feel during and after the interaction.

If your purpose is to make sure Ted likes you, then this is going to produce a very different experience than if you want to know what Ted did last weekend. Or perhaps you know that Ted knows a lot about windsurfing, which you happen to find quite interesting. If you want to pick his brain about a topic, then your purpose is very different than if you were seeking his approval. Or perhaps you think Ted is pretty funny and the last time you talked with him he made you laugh. In this case, your purpose might be to share some banter, be playful, and have a good laugh. Each one of those purposes is going to produce a very different set of feelings inside of you.

Much of the time, when we experience social anxiety and come to fear interactions, it is because we have not chosen or defined our desired outcome. Or, it is because the desired outcome we've chosen does not serve us.

Below are questions we frequently ask ourselves before a social interaction:

- How can I get this person to like me?
- How can I make sure that they think I'm okay?
- How can I get through this without embarrassing myself?

Depending on the question, your purpose might be to avoid embarrassment, to receive approval, or to get a positive response from another person. It is true that most of us prefer when people like us, we generally want to avoid embarrassment, and we usually want positive responses from others. It is important, however, to make sure these are not our *only* desired outcomes.

Changing your question, choosing your purpose

Once you become aware of what your purpose is in a given moment, you can determine whether or not it is serving you. If, for example, you realize that your outcome whenever you speak to an attractive woman is to get her to approve of you, then you now know more about yourself and why you might feel anxious in those situations. Before your next interaction, or any other activity, take the time to ask yourself, "What is my purpose? What is my desired outcome here?"

This does not mean you are a robot, or that all interactions are some sort of transaction where you only want to get things out of people. Your purpose could simply be to enjoy yourself, to fully listen to another person and hear about her life, or to share something interesting with someone else. Your purpose could be vulnerability and authenticity, or to tell the other person how you honestly feel. Notice how these types of outcomes are not manipulative. In reality, they are often mutually beneficial. When your purpose is focused on the other person, or on connecting, you will most likely be more present and able to relate to them in a relaxed, confident manner.

A great way to change your purpose from one that is disempowering (e.g. avoiding embarrassment) to one that is empowering (e.g. getting to know another person) is to ask yourself better guiding questions. These questions will determine your purpose for an interaction. Consider some of the typical guiding questions shy people have:

● What will they think of me?
● Is she going to reject me?
● What if I run out of things to say?

These questions guide your focus towards what you do *not* want to occur, and reveal goals of gaining approval, avoiding rejection, and avoiding judgment and criticism. Alternatively, what questions might lead to more empowering purposes? Can you come up with any? What could you ask yourself that would help guide your outcome towards something that you want? Hint: The best purpose questions often start with "how" or "what."

Did you come up with any? Here are a few examples to add to your list:

● How can I help this person feel at ease?
● What do I like about this person?
● How can I connect even more with this person?
● What does this person really need right now?
● How can I give and receive even more love right now?

What outcomes are operating behind these questions? Your outcome might be to help someone feel at ease, to identify and share positive things you notice about another, to connect, to meet someone's needs, or to give and receive love. Not only do these questions guide your focus away from anxiety-producing worries about rejection, but they also change your entire purpose behind the interaction. The next time you talk with a stranger, meet up with a friend or girlfriend, interact with a co-worker, or even go to the gym, stop and ask yourself, "What is my purpose?"

Your life purpose

Each of us has a deeper purpose that goes beyond our daily activities. Our purpose influences our behavior, thoughts, feelings, and actions, and it also taps into something much deeper and closer to our cores. While this philosophical question might seem beyond the scope of this book, I believe it is incredibly important for you to have a sense of your purpose. You can begin with a hunch or a guess. As you keep exploring this you will gain more clarity over time.

Nothing is more grounding, rooting, or strengthening than knowing who you are, what you are about, and what you are doing here. A great way to do this is to ask yourself, "Why am I here? What is my purpose?"

At first, these types of questions might seem too big to answer. *How could I possibly know?* One simple way to break things down is to realize that your purpose does not need to be some grand mission or monumental achievement, such as being the first human on Mars or making a billion dollars. These types of extremes are more akin to "goals" than to a "purpose." The purpose of your life is not to earn X amount of dollars, gain some accolade, or even to marry and have children. Those are all goals—things you may desire and strive towards, but certainly not your purpose.

Your life purpose is not a goal or an end result. It is a way of being in the world. Your purpose is a verb. It describes who you want to be, how you want to be, what you want to create, give, and contribute to the world while you are here.

Here is a purpose I came up with for myself a little over a year ago. It is still working well for me, so I am sticking to it:

The purpose of my life is to unconditionally love and accept myself; to be real, authentic, and genuine; to be playful, creative, courageous, outrageous, silly, and fun; to make people laugh and smile; to teach them how to love and accept themselves, and to have the courage and passion to pursue their dreams.

Each time I say it, I get fired up. I like it so much I've committed it to memory, and I remind myself of it several times per week.

Now, what is *your* life purpose?

Read the following sentences out loud and fill in the blank with whatever comes to your mind. Do not overanalyze or overthink. Simply blurt out the first thing that sounds good to you.

The purpose of my life is to _____

The purpose of my life is to **be** _____

I am here to **enjoy** _____

I am here to **share** _____

What did you come up with? What words came to mind when you were describing *who* and *how* you want to be in the world? Your responses reflect what you value—the traits, attitudes, attributes and actions that are most important to you. These are different than specific goals and end results. Instead of being a destination, values create a compass that guides you in your daily life.

Take the time to write out a purpose for yourself, like the example provided above. Yours might be longer or shorter than mine, and it may contain entirely different content. The most important thing is that reading it fills you with a sense of passion, satisfaction, meaning, or fulfillment. Once you have crafted a purpose, which is always a work in progress, you can read it to yourself regularly. It becomes that much more powerful when you take the time and energy to memorize it. This allows you to access it any time you need to.

Knowing your life purpose keeps you connected to what you value most. It can help you when you are facing a difficult decision, and are unsure about how to proceed. It can help you remain grounded after a fight or uncomfortable interaction. Instead of spiraling off into self-criticism or anxiety, you can remind yourself of who you are, and what you are really about.

Seven

ACCEPT YOURSELF...*ALL* OF YOURSELF.

By now you are quite familiar with the basic assumption that lies behind all social anxiety. *On some level I am not good enough, I am not going to be accepted, I am unacceptable.* In fact, you probably know it by heart. That repetition is not designed to annoy you. Rather, it is actually part of the learning process to help you realize that the source of social anxiety is simply a belief...a perception...an idea. And an idea is something that can be changed.

When we believe we are not good enough, we identify parts of ourselves—thoughts, feelings, behaviors, aspects of our physical appearance, etc.—and judge those parts as unacceptable. We find them unappealing, gross, disgusting, irritating, or otherwise wrong in some way. We then tend to assume that other people think the same way, and that they also see those parts of us as gross and unacceptable. We do what psychologists call *projection.* This is when we project our own internal ideas and feelings onto others, assuming they are thinking and feeling the same way. *I don't like the way my body looks, therefore you must dislike the way my body looks.*

In addition, we all have the tendency to see what we are expecting to see. We expect other people will reject us, and so we start to anticipate and see rejections in all of our interactions. In other words, we find what we seek. Our mind starts to look for evidence that people think little of us, judge us, and perceive us as not smart enough, tall enough, attractive enough, etc. We see an ambiguous gesture like a crinkled brow, or a quizzical look, and we immediately conclude that they do not like us, that we are unacceptable. In this way, we continually find evidence to support the belief that we are not good enough, which further convinces us that others will reject us. When we do not like ourselves, when we are rejecting many parts of ourselves, it can be hard to imagine that others can accept us. When people do seem to like us, we can find all kinds of ways to discount their opinion. We might say "they're just pretending to be nice because they feel sorry for me." Then we can withdraw from them, which allows us to maintain the belief that we are unacceptable. This, in turn, keeps our social anxiety alive.

This chapter is devoted to helping you shift your pattern of negative self-judgment, along with the persistent fear that others are judging you negatively. As you start to change your relationship with yourself, you will find it has a profound impact on how you feel, and on how others respond to you. The first step to creating a better relationship with yourself is to become aware of how you might be rejecting parts of yourself on a daily basis.

AWARENESS

Are you aware of what goes on in your mind throughout the day? Most of us are unfortunately *too* aware of all of our thoughts, reactions, and worries in response to our lives. However, there is one kind of experience that tends to be overlooked. It is a pattern of thinking that is so common, so ordinary, and so familiar, that we may not even notice it after a while. It is like the whir of an air-conditioner—we eventually tune it out and forget it exists.

This pattern is at the root of negative feelings about yourself, and it keeps you stuck in a place of low self-worth and self-esteem. In order to make any headway on the path towards social confidence, you must gain awareness of this pattern, and make consistent efforts to change it.

MEET YOUR CRITIC

For every person on this planet, there appears to be an individual critic tailored just for him or her. Perhaps someone like the Dalai Lama has overcome this challenge, but every person I have met deals with their inner critic on a regular basis. What is the critic? It is that voice in your head, that internal string of thoughts that is judging you and finding you inadequate, bad or wrong. It tells you that you are not good looking enough, that you said something stupid, or that you are pathetic for feeling anxious.

The first, and most powerful, way to shift the process of being hard on yourself is to become more and more aware of it as it is happening. Let me give you some examples so you can start to understand your critic.

Tim is a tall, thin, bright young man who is about to go to a dinner party with a friend. Other than his friend and one mutual acquaintance, the rest of the people will be strangers. He has been practicing being more social recently, and he hopes to make some more friends. He even hopes that he might meet a cute, single girl.

Once he accepted the invitation and hung up the phone, however, he started to feel a little anxious. He started to think, *oh my god, this is going to be uncomfortable. I won't know anyone there. This is going to be so awkward. People won't want to talk with me. I'm so boring. I have nothing good to wear, all my clothes are so old and lame. My hair is terrible.*

Long before he gets to the party, his inner critic has begun its campaign. By the time he arrives, how do you imagine he is feeling if his critic has been active all day?

When Tim and his friend arrive at the party, sure enough he sees six or seven people he has never met. His heart starts beating, and his mind begins to race. Enter his critic: *I'm terrible at meeting people. I never know what to say. It's going to be really awkward and uncomfortable.*

Once he gets into the house, he makes a beeline for the table with the wine and beer. He pours himself some wine and stands near the table, slowing sipping from his glass. In his mind he hears, *God, look at you. You're standing here so awkwardly. You should be talking to someone. What's wrong with you? People notice that you're not talking to anyone. They're going to think you're a freak. What's wrong with you? You better look busy, people are going to think you're just lurking in the corner.*

How is he feeling now? He is undoubtedly feeling quite tense and awkward. He is having a terrible time all because this critic is running rampant inside of his mind. Shortly thereafter, an attractive young woman walks to the table to pour herself a drink. Tim is standing within several feet. She looks up at him and smiles for a moment. He gives a quick, strained smile, which looks more like a grimace, and quickly averts his eyes. His critic jumps into high gear: *What the hell is wrong with you? Say something to her! Don't just stand there like a total idiot! Come on, say something!*

Under the compelling attack of his own internal monologue, Tim moves towards the woman and initiates a conversation.

"Hey, how's it going? I'm Tim." He says with a smile as he extends his hand.

"Hi Tim, I'm Audrey," she responds while returning the handshake.

"So, um, what are you drinking?"

As Tim begins to converse with Audrey, his inner critic continues to harass him: *That was awkward. Why did you say that? That was stupid. You looked away when she was talking.*

She's going to think that you're not interested in what she's saying.
You need to get out of this interaction as quickly as possible. You're
making a fool of yourself.

Can you relate to this experience? This is incredibly common for people who struggle with debilitating shyness or social anxiety. Notice how Tim's critic attacks him before and during the party. What happens after he leaves? Does the critic ease up?

Eventually, after a long, grueling evening, his friend drops Tim off and he crawls into bed, exhausted. Unfortunately, sleep does not come easily this night. In the quiet of the early morning hours, his critic kicks into high gear: *What the hell is wrong with me? This is never going to work. I'm never going to be able to be comfortable around people. I've always felt this way. There must be something terribly wrong with me.*

Tim wakes up the next morning feeling sad and discouraged. He has yet more evidence that he cannot be social, reinforcing his negative beliefs, fears, and social anxieties.

INTERNAL TYRANNY

What is happening for Tim? What is happening for all of us when we struggle with an insatiable and relentless inner critic? Essentially, we each have an internal critic that is convinced that we are not good enough. This critic is convinced that because we are not good enough, no one is going to like us, and we are going to get rejected. Since this is bound to happen, it is better to play it safe and *to avoid.*

- Avoid risks.
- Avoid putting ourselves out there.
- Avoid interacting with others.
- Avoid anything that could lead to further rejection, pain, or failure.

Your critic believes this so strongly, that it will say *anything* to stop you from taking a risk. Buying into the critic's narrative, we believe we have to be cautious, reserved, and careful to not make a mistake or offend anyone, ever. Staying small and being self-critical feels pretty bad, but it is better than throwing ourselves into the unknown and potentially experiencing much worse things like rejection, external criticism, or ridicule. Does this type of agreement remind you of anything?

I will take complete control here and tell you what to do and what not to do. If you disobey me I will make you suffer. I am doing this to keep you safe. There are much greater threats outside of here that you need my help to avoid.

That sounds awfully similar to the Mafia's "protection" or a tyrannical dictatorship. Much like a national tyranny, our inner tyranny uses a heavy propaganda campaign to influence us. The message is shared regularly, across all situations, with volume, intensity, and massive repetition.

Isn't your inner critic's message loud? When you are about to do something risky or scary, such as give a spontaneous toast in front of a group, doesn't it take on a high volume, yelling tone? The critic in your mind is also highly repetitive. It can repeat the same catchy slogans dozens of times per day, loading them with more and more significance:

- There's something wrong with you.
- You are awkward.
- You are a loser.

It can say things 10, 15, 20 times or more per day, depending on how badly you're struggling. That is an incredible amount of repetition. If something is repeated long enough, loud enough, and frequently enough, it will stick. The things your critic says to you might be things you have been listening to for years, or even decades. This repetition can make it seem incredibly convincing. In this way, a lie can start to feel true. This is exactly what is happening. You are experiencing an internal propaganda campaign. Just like living under an oppressive tyrannical dictatorship, the only way to gain liberation is to strongly commit to breaking free. This does not mean murdering your inner critic, eradicating it, or banishing it forever. While this is something we might wish we could do after years of being bullied, unfortunately your critic is here to stay. However, it does not have to be in charge, and it does not have to torment you so much.

Your task, which the following sections will help you accomplish, is to learn to work with this part of yourself so that you can heed its warnings and fears while still being free to act how you truly want to act. Essentially, it is learning how to *not believe* it as much. It might still be there, but it no longer has as much power over you. In other words, the dictator is some old guy on a bench playing chess, rather than the absolute ruler of your internal environment.

Catching Your Critic

The first step to *de-fanging* your inner critic is to gain an acute awareness of what you are saying to yourself on a regular basis. Gaining awareness is an integral part of the transformation that can occur through meditation practices and modern psychotherapies, such as cognitive behavioral therapy.

It is essential to become *aware* of what our critic is saying. Before we become aware, we tend to believe what the critic says without even realizing it's the critic speaking, and not us. In other words, your critic might be so persistent and familiar that you believe the voice you're hearing is actually how you truly think about things—that the critic is *who you are.*

Awareness will allow you to notice the critic, label it as such, and realize that it is the propaganda campaign. Without this, what the critic says might just seem true. A thought such as, *I am so awkward that no one would ever want to date me,* might seem as true and factual as a thought that says, *I am hungry,* or, *it's 72 degrees out today.*

When people have been fed propaganda for an extended period of time, they no longer recognize it as propaganda. In order to see the propaganda for what it is—a lie based on fear— you must wake up.

The Awareness Log

Below is an exercise called an Awareness Log. Completing this exercise regularly can have a powerful effect on your ability to notice when you are being self-critical, and help you begin to change this pattern. Completing it is simple. Once you know how to do it, it only takes a few minutes.

How to complete the Awareness Log:

1. Pick a situation that you find yourself anxious, down, frustrated, afraid, or upset about. Write the situation at the top of the page. You do not need to go into great detail here—a simple one-sentence description is all you need.

2. Check in to see how you are feeling about the situation. When we are experiencing negative emotions, we sometimes only know we are feeling "bad." Review the emotions listed in the Log and circle the ones that describe how you are feeling in response to the situation you described above.

3. Pause for a moment and take a few breaths, paying close attention to what is happening in your body. Do you feel tightness in your throat? Tears behind your eyes? Shaky

hands? A clenched jaw? Write down a few sentences describing the physical sensations you notice.

4. In the section entitled "Automatic Thoughts," write down the thoughts that are going through your mind about the situation, especially the ones that are self-critical, fearful, depressing, or hurtful. These are the thoughts we automatically have, without choosing them consciously.

5. Pause for a moment, take several deep breaths. You can even put the sheet of paper down for a minute and stand up to shake your body out. Changing your body can help you start to change your patterns of thought. In the final section of this exercise, write down responses to each of your negative, harsh or critical thoughts. Try using alternatives that are more compassionate, more realistic, and more optimistic.

Below you will find an example that will help you more fully understand how to use the Awareness Log in your daily life. This tool is incredibly beneficial, especially when it is used regularly. When I am working with a client, I will often recommend they complete one Awareness Log per day for two weeks. This regular use starts to train your mind to perceive your thoughts and feelings more clearly. After doing this for just several days, you will start to notice yourself "catching" the propaganda of your self-critic and naturally finding alternative ways of viewing the situation that are more self-compassionate and realistic.

You will find a blank awareness log below to make photocopies to use over the next few weeks. You can also download a free version from the website (www.socialconfidencecenter.com/awareness-log).

A note about your critic: In the examples below, and throughout this section, you will notice the voice of the critic can be in the first person (e.g. "I am no good"), or in the 2nd person (e.g. "You are no good"). You might experience your critic in one or both of these ways. Use whichever language most accurately reflects how your critic speaks to you.

Awareness Log

Situation (describe):

I made a joke during the break at work, and no one laughed.

Emotions (circle):

(Anxious)	(Inadequate)	Angry	Lonely	Guilty
Worried	Inferior	Frustrated	Unloved	Ashamed
Nervous	(Worthless)	Hopeless	(Embarrassed)	(Discouraged)

Body Sensations (describe):

I feel a squeezing in my throat. My chest feels tight and it's hard to take in a deep breath. I also feel a hollow empty feeling in my stomach.

Automatic Thoughts	Alternatives
That was so stupid. Why did I say that?	I was joining in the joking, and I was just having a good time.
Everyone there thinks I'm an idiot.	This is extreme. Some people might be upset, others probably didn't even notice.
They're all talking about me and making fun of me.	It seems unlikely that they have nothing better to do than make fun of me!
I am not funny. Why do I try to make jokes?	I'm actually a pretty funny guy. No one makes jokes that everyone laughs at every time.
No wonder I don't have any friends. I'm such a loser.	Just because I said something and people didn't laugh does not mean I am bad or unlikeable. Everyone has a few bombs— even great comedians.

Awareness Log

Situation (describe):

Emotions (circle):

Anxious	Inadequate	Angry	Lonely	Guilty
Worried	Inferior	Frustrated	Unloved	Ashamed
Nervous	Worthless	Hopeless	Embarrassed	Discouraged

Body Sensations (describe):

Automatic Thoughts	Alternatives

Mapping the board room

Another powerful way to gain awareness of your inner critic is to view it as a character, or a part of yourself. We tend to assume that we are a single person, but when we start to examine our minds, it becomes clear that we have all kinds of differing desires, thoughts, and feelings inside of us.

Rather than being a single entity, you can view yourself as a collection of different parts. Part of you wants to eat a pizza, and part of you wants to get the salad because it is healthier. Part of you hopes something will go well, and another part is paralyzed by fear of failure. In working with these parts of ourselves, it can be helpful to imagine that inside your head there is a corporate boardroom. There's a large wooden table with many plush leather chairs, and around the table are all different parts of you. You are the head of the board, the arbiter of the discussion. It is your job to hear from each part, as well as to keep order and prevent one part from hijacking the entire meeting.

When dealing with your critic in this manner, it can be helpful to imagine your critic as just another character in this boardroom. Additionally, it can help to give your critic a name or title. This not only helps you label and catch it quicker, it also helps you take some of the charge out of what it is saying by giving it a playful or silly name. For example, when I am dealing with my inner critic, I call him Admiral Doom. He is the bringer of nothing but bad news and he predicts that anything I try will fail and that I am, well...doomed.

I have identified other parts as well. The part of me that is terribly frightened that something might go wrong in the future is The Blind Prophet. The part that is convinced everyone will dislike me because I won't meet their expectations is Double More—it always demands I do more. When I ask Double More just *how much more* I should do, it always says "double!" The list goes on.

It can be incredibly helpful to start to notice, identify, and name the different parts of yourself, especially your inner critic. Once you have done this, you can playfully call out who is in charge of the meeting. "Admiral Doom? Who put you in charge? You'll steer this whole company into the ground!"

Many clients I have worked with have actually found it helpful to make a sketch or cartoon drawing of their internal boardroom, including the names of all the characters within it. This is a more playful, non-linear, right-brained way to become more aware of your inner critic. You can experiment with both this and the Awareness Log to help you grow more familiar with this part of yourself.

CHALLENGING THE CRITIC

As you learned in the previous section, the first step to breaking free from the clutches of your inner critic is to gain awareness of it. That includes recognizing, labeling, and even naming your critic.

Have you named your critic yet? What is it?

"My inner critic is called my inner critic."

That is a start, but the more playful and creative you are with this process, the more it will help you get free from your critic.

When you name your critic, you tell your subconscious that the critic is not you. This reinforces that the harsh, negative thoughts are simply ideas in your mind. They do not reflect clear facts or the whole truth. In fact, as you have done the Awareness Logs, you may have realized that many of your critical thoughts are quite distorted or inaccurate. Once you realize this, you can start to make a distinction between having a thought and believing it.

We are always having thoughts. Some are clear, linear, and relevant to what is happening around us. Others are out of left field, random, or off the wall. Once we see this, we realize that we do not need to believe every thought that goes through our minds. Some of them are downright ridiculous! We can stop buying into all of our thoughts, assuming they are *all* accurate, *all* true, and *all* clearly reflect reality. Once we realize that we do not have to buy into every thought we have, a powerful shift starts to take place. One way to accelerate this shift is to actively challenge our self-critical thoughts.

Challenging With Questions

Questions are an incredibly influential form of communication between people and even within our own minds. Great teachers understand that students gain tremendous insight and knowledge simply through being asked a series of questions.

The example below illustrates a common scenario for those who struggle with social anxiety, while the questions that follow will help you challenge an over-active inner critic.

Imagine you spent the evening having dinner with several people. Some are friends or coworkers, and others are people you don't know very well. On your way home from dinner, your critic starts to act up.

You got too excited when you were talking about skiing. You sounded like such a dork. You were over the top, way too excited. They didn't really enjoy being around you, they were just tolerating you. Your relationships are worse than ever. No one really likes you. No one really wants to be around you.

This is a pretty intense barrage of critical propaganda. Are these thoughts completely accurate and true? Not necessarily, but it can be hard to stand up to this kind of attack. In fact, this type of thinking can be so compelling, and seem so true, that we get stuck in a trance. The pattern goes like this:

- The thoughts arise in a repetitive, convincing fashion.
- We believe them and feel bad about ourselves.
- Soon, the thoughts—mixed with our negative emotions— begin to reinforce all the underlying negative thoughts that persistently dog us.
- Deflated and defeated, we no longer feel like hanging out with these people for fear of rejection.

The best way to break the trance is to start asking yourself specific questions that will help you see the situation clearly.

What is the truth?

When your critic launches an attack against you, it can seem incredibly convincing. So much so that many people just accept whatever their critic says as accurate. Part of this is due to the familiarity of the critic's voice, and part is because of how *certain* your critic sounds. Your critic does not typically put forth a tentative hypothesis for you to check out. On the contrary, it loudly asserts a claim as if it were absolute truth.

They don't like you. You suck. Something's wrong with you.

Here are some truth-based questions you can ask yourself in order to gain some space from these internal attacks:

Truth-Based Questions
• Do I know for certain that they didn't like being around me?
• Is that *absolutely*, certainly true?
• Can I know that with 100% certainty?

Softening extremes

As you pay attention to your critic more carefully over time, you may start to notice it has a tendency to speak in extremes and absolutes, using words like "always," "never," "nobody," "everybody," etc.

- **Nobody** likes you because you have **nothing** to offer.
- I **always** make a fool of myself when I try to start a conversation with a stranger.
- **No one** will **ever** want to go out with me because I'm such a loser.

While we might make statements like this in our everyday life, are they really true? These *overgeneralizations* occur when we take a specific situation—e.g., someone doesn't want to go out with me—and transform it into a general rule about the world. Now, instead of *one person* not being interested, *no one* will *ever* want to date me! A bit extreme, isn't it?

Unfortunately, while these claims are quite exaggerated, they can feel true when your critic is yelling them in your head. A great way to start to break this pattern is to ask things that challenge the extreme nature of these statements. Going back to the dinner party example, pay attention to the extreme nature of the thoughts:

They didn't really enjoy being around you, they were just tolerating you. Your relationships now are worse than ever. No one really likes you. No one wants to be around you.

In response, you can ask yourself questions like these:

Questions to Soften Extremes

- Does *every* single person from the group dislike being around me?
- How much of the time?
- Did they like being around me for part of the night, but then not when I was talking about skiing?
- Do they *totally* dislike *all* of me as a person?

The point of these questions is to undermine the extreme nature of your critic's propaganda campaign. As with any propaganda, when someone holds the questioning light of truth up to it, you can see how over-the-top the claims really are.

Examining the evidence

In addition to being over-generalized and extreme, your critic's claims are often based on vague, inconclusive evidence. Like a prosecuting attorney with a weak case, your critic will attempt to convict you using nothing but hearsay and speculation.

One way to undermine this pattern is to explore the actual evidence your critic is using. The following questions can help you *cross-examine* the specifics:

Questions to Examine the Evidence

- How am I coming to this conclusion?
- What evidence do I have that they did not like me?
- What specifically did I *see* or *hear* that gives me this idea?

Frequently, something insignificant happens, yet we pick up on it as a sign of boredom, disapproval, or dislike. Perhaps when you ask yourself the questions above, you discover that when you were talking about skiing during dinner, a guy named Jim made several jokes.

"Whoa, you are really into this."

You might also remember that when you were talking, a girl named Tina looked down for a while, leading you to conclude that she was disinterested in what you were saying.

It's easy for us to convince ourselves that our conclusions are accurate, and that any attempt to see things otherwise is just a deluded stab at making ourselves feel better.

Face the facts, your critic says. *You are boring and they don't like you. Quit trying to kid yourself.*

This is referred to as *emotional reasoning,* and is a way your critic can overwhelm you. In essence, it occurs when you conclude something is true based solely on a *strong feeling* that it is true.

I am a total loser, because I feel like a total loser.

This criticism is difficult to challenge because it is based on some very circular logic. When you notice you are doing this, take a step back and look at what is actually happening in the situation. You might even start to question your conclusions about Jim and Tina's actions, motivations, etc., and whether or not their actions *mean something* other than what you've concluded.

What else could this mean?

Let's examine the evidence for why Jim and Tina do not like you.

- Jim made jokes.
- Tina looked down as you spoke.

Your mind immediately concludes that the reason they acted this way is because they did not like you. What's more, you have a strong feeling that you are unlikeable, which your critic uses as further evidence that you are indeed an unlovable wretch. But what if the meaning you give things is based more on your fears and assumptions, than what is *really* happening? Remember the exercise where you searched for red in the room? When we are subconsciously searching for the ways people do not like us, or are bored with us, then we will find evidence to prove this assumption.

A great way to break that pattern is to ask yourself, "What else could this mean?" In this instance, what else could it mean that Jim was making jokes and Tina looked down? How else can we interpret their actions? Does someone looking away *automatically* mean that they do not like you *as a person?* Could it be that they were thinking about something else? Could it be that maybe they *are* a little bit bored, but that it is no big deal? Aren't you sometimes a little bored when a friend is telling you something? Does it mean you hate them and never want to hang out with them again?

Let's take a moment to go with the fear. Suppose that when you noticed Jim and Tina's actions, they *were* a little bored. What is the worst that could happen? Take a moment to imagine it. Sometimes going with our fears and taking them to their logical conclusions can have a calming effect.

What is the worst possible thing that could happen because they were bored?

Most likely the worst scenario you came up with is they no longer want to spend time with you, and do not return your calls or emails. They reject you. While this might be painful, especially if you like them, would it be *unbearable?* Would it mean you are a completely unlovable person? Is it possible you might not be the best match for each other, and that you could find friends who are equally enthused about skiing? Do their opinions in the moment reflect those of everyone else on the planet?

Isn't it amazing how quickly we can generalize, going from a specific instance to *everyone, everywhere?* We tell ourselves,

"Well, if this person isn't interested in *that*, then no one is interested in *that*. I must be a boring person." But what if you were talking to someone who was an equally avid, excited skier? They might even want to talk about skiing more than you do.

Getting perspective

Have you noticed that when we believe someone does not like us, it can feel like a terrible crisis? It feels like something we absolutely have to figure out, or change immediately because it is so uncomfortable. It is amazing how wrapped up we get in this sense of fear. It can be so consuming that we go into a trance of negative thoughts and feelings. We become convinced that someone does not like us, and that we are unlikeable.

This cycle is one of tremendous suffering, and can make the idea of maintaining perspective quite challenging. The following questions can help you maintain a sense of perspective during these challenging moments:

Questions to Gain Perspective
• Is whether this person likes me or not so important that my entire future depends on this?
• Is it really true that everything hinges on this?
• Who else loves me in my life?
• Whom do I love?

A final way to gain perspective is to take note of how you are thinking, and determine if it is helping or hurting you. When you buy the thought *they don't like me, I was too excited and no one wants to be around me,* how do you feel? Does it make you feel better or worse? If worse, then perhaps there is a different way to view the situation that might make you feel better.

Hidden assumptions

In addition to asking yourself questions, you can defend against your critic by examining your *hidden assumptions* about yourself and the world around you. These assumptions are often unconscious, yet lurk behind every interaction. The more aware of them you become, the less ammunition your critic will have when it launches attacks against you.

Hidden assumptions are beliefs or rules you have about how you are *supposed* to be, how conversations are *supposed* to go, how others are *supposed* to relate to you, etc. In the example above, there might be many hidden assumptions at work.

Do you assume that no one should *ever* feel bored with *anything* that you say? That everyone should be *completely* entertained *all* the time? Do you feel the need to be entertaining? If you were not entertaining, would people not have a reason or desire to hang out with you? Perhaps you have the hidden assumption that people should never look away when you are talking, or that you should never disagree with someone.

These assumptions help compensate for the basic fear that there is something wrong with you, and you have to work extra hard to make sure people like you. You have to be extra entertaining, an incredible listener, always loving and patient, attentive and agreeable no matter what, and so forth. These rules for yourself turn into hidden assumptions. When someone breaks one of them, you conclude they do not like you.

What are your hidden assumptions? This is a great question to reflect on before and after conversations, or in situations where you feel anxious or embarrassed.

So, what are your hidden expectations for yourself and others?

DIALOGUING WITH YOUR CRITIC

You must identify and challenge your critic before you can develop social confidence. While being able to counter your critic is a powerful way to feel more liberated, it can sometimes be an uphill battle. You might find that you get into long debates in your mind, as if a prosecutor and a defense attorney are arguing about whether or not you are a good person. This can make you feel like you are at odds with yourself and produce even more suffering.

While it might sound abrasive and harsh, your critic is actually a very scared, vulnerable part of you. Even though your critic seems tough, chances are it is terrified of something such as failure or rejection. To that end, the practice of dialoguing with your critic can be very powerful in helping you achieve a sense of peace and integration.

How To Talk With Yourself

The idea of talking with yourself might seem a little strange at first. However, once you learn more about it, and how it can help you, you might find it starts to feel more natural. Besides, when your critic is haranguing you, you are already talking to yourself. You might as well do it consciously and take some control of the process.

When speaking with your critic, it is incredibly useful to get the process out of your head, either onto paper, or through actual conversation. You can keep a journal of your thoughts, or if you are working with a counselor, or are comfortable enlisting a close friend, you can have the person play the part of your critic so you can dialogue out loud. Once you start to see or hear this dialogue, you will recognize how extreme, unrealistic, or even ridiculous your critic might be.

There are three ways to respond to your critic that you might find particularly helpful: defense, questioning, and acceptance. The first way is to directly challenge your critic, saying something like: "I disagree. That seems extreme. I'm not sure that is true." The second way to respond is to ask your critic questions that highlight his logic. You can also ask for specifics when he is making a vague or extreme claim. For example:

Critic: No one likes you.
Me: No one? Do you mean nobody at all, or just this person?

A final way to respond to your critic is by flowing with the attacks and finding a grain of truth in them. This is a powerful form of acceptance that allows you to acknowledge a shortcoming or mistake, without taking on the meaning that you are a bad person because of it. The general attitude behind the acceptance is: *Yes, I make mistakes and have flaws, but I am still a good person who is worthy of love and belonging.*

A conversation with yourself

Below is a sample dialogue between a person and his critic. When you are doing this exercise on your own, you can write out a dialogue just like this one. One of the main purposes is to gain a greater understanding of your critic. On some level, it is scared and angry. What does your critic fear? What does it want from you? Is there any way you can calm your critic down to the point where it works with you, rather than against you?

The following transcript is based on the example above (the interaction with Jim and Tina). See if you can identify how the speaker uses the three strategies—defense, questioning, and acceptance. You may also notice how the purpose of the dialogue is to increase understanding, connection, and cooperation between these two different parts of yourself.

Critic: Oh my god, that was so stupid. You were so awkward there. You talked way too much.

Response: Well, I do like to get going on downhill skiing. Sometimes I can really get into it.

Critic: This is no joking matter. I mean, it was annoying. People were annoyed with you.

Response: I don't know if that's fully true. It didn't seem like people were annoyed. It seemed like Carl and Jeff were listening and interested. For the most part it was a pretty normal conversation. I was sharing something that I'm interested in.

Critic: Well, that's bullshit because Jim was making all those jokes about how excited you were, and Tina was looking away as you were talking.

Response: Yeah, Jim did make a few jokes and Tina did seem like she was looking away. What do you think that means, that Jim was making those jokes?

Critic: I think it means that he thinks you're a freak, and too excited, and kind of a joke.

Response: *(Laughs)* Well, that's really extreme. Jim seemed pretty friendly. I don't know if he'd be having such harsh, critical thoughts. That might just be what you are saying. I don't really know if I have evidence that Jim believes that. And besides, I was excited, and I think it's okay for me to talk about things I'm excited about.

Critic: Well sure, you can talk about what you were excited about, but Tina was just looking off into space, because you're so boring. Everyone thinks that you're boring.

Response: *Everyone?* Is that really true? I mean, it seems like there were a number of people that found me interesting. I really don't think I can generalize from Tina to everybody.

Critic: Yeah, well, I'm afraid so. You're just so boring and annoying...I hate you.

Response: Wow, it sounds like you're upset with me right now. It sounds like you're angry about something. Why are you angry with me?

Critic: I'm angry with you because those people didn't like you, and it pisses me off. I want you to be different, I want you to be better.

Response: Okay, you're really upset. You want me to be different than I am. It sounds like you might be scared or something.

Critic: I'm not scared, I just don't like you. I think you suck.

Response: Okay, so you're obviously really upset. What do you want for me? It sounds like you want me to be different. What would I change if I were different?

Critic: Well, I would want you to be confident, and I want people to like you. I want you to be able to get a date, and get into a relationship and all that stuff.

Response: Really? Wow, I didn't know you wanted those things. I want those things too.

Critic: Yeah, well, you're not going to get those things if you're boring.

Response: Oh, so you are worried that if I bore people, then I'm not going to find a partner, or no one's going to want to date me. Is that what you're worried about?

Critic: Yeah. I think you really have to watch that. Or else no one's going to want to be around us.

Response: I see. It sounds like you're scared. It sounds like you really want us to be able to have a relationship, and to find a partner.

Critic: Yeah, that's what I want.

Response: Well, I want that too. But, the way you're going about it doesn't make me feel more confident. It makes me terrified to go to parties or meet people, because I'm going to get beaten by you afterwards. I'm wondering if there's a better way to respond to these situations, so that I can build up my confidence and feel good about myself.

Critic: Yeah, but if I let up on you then you're just going to be this annoying, talkative person and no one's ever going to want to be around us.

Response: You seem really convinced of that. I agree that we don't want to push people away by being over-talkative, but I think that I've got to try to be myself and trust that people are going to like me for who I am, whether I'm excited, tired, or anything else. I can't be on and perfect all the time. Besides, that was really important to me. We really like skiing, don't we?

Critic: Yeah, I guess.

Response: So, can you be more compassionate? Can you be a little more patient? Can you encourage me a little more? That might help me to get to what we want. Maybe we can take a risk and see. Let's see if those people want to hang out again.

Critic: Okay.

What did you notice reading this dialogue? What did you learn about how to speak with your own critic? What fears were lurking behind the critic's attacks?

Did you notice how when you empathize with the critic, and stay with it, it can start to calm down? In many ways, this wound-up, self-critical part of us is simply having a tantrum. It might seem all-powerful and intimidating, but it is just like a young child throwing an aggressive tantrum. If you can stay with this part, listen to it, empathize with it, and not buy its story, you might find it calms down quite a bit.

I highly encourage you to write out a dialogue of your own on a regular basis. For a period of several months, I wrote out one dialogue per night in a journal. I've experienced some of my greatest feelings of inner peace and joy when my critic and I were aligned after a long conversation. When we finally stop being at odds with ourselves, something profoundly relaxing happens in our minds and bodies.

SELF-COMPASSION

The skills described above—challenging the critic, talking with it, disagreeing with it, accepting it—are all incredibly useful, and must be cultivated in order to overcome social anxiety. Sometimes, however, you might feel like you are arguing with yourself, like you are just getting nowhere. For every response you have, the critic has a better, more powerful, more evidenced-based response that you just cannot challenge. No matter how much evidence or how many challenges you provide, the critic seems to beat you down.

Other times you are just feeling so worn down, so tired, so low, that you do not have the energy to write out a dialogue or try to challenge your inner critic. When this happens, the most useful thing you can do is to actually stop fighting the critic. Instead of focusing more effort on what is not working, you can direct your attention towards giving yourself unconditional self-compassion.

In the cycle described above, there is an attack, then a defense, then a better, fiercer attack. This circuit of self-criticism can feed on itself endlessly. The more you try to fight your critic, the stronger and more convincing it gets. Self-compassion can help *break the circuit.*

FINDING THE HIDDEN VULNERABILITY

As you may have learned from dialoguing with your critic, self-attack usually comes in response to something we fear, or a *disowned tenderness* we don't want to feel. The fear that people might not like us makes us feel very vulnerable. Just the idea that we need other people to love us in this life, and that we cannot control their feelings, can leave us feeling vulnerable. Sharing what we are excited or hopeful about can make us feel exposed.

Sharing our dreams and visions for what we want to do and who we hope to become is incredibly sensitive and tender.

This vulnerability is a natural and necessary part of being a healthy, loving person. But our critic does not like us being vulnerable. When you were younger, perhaps members of your family or peer group picked on you. One of your parents may have been absent, or worse, actively abusive. In those tough circumstances, there is a part of you that concludes that being vulnerable is bad. It means you will get hurt.

Enter the critic. It tries to protect you from vulnerability in two ways. First, it tells you that sharing this with another person is a bad idea—you should just keep it to yourself. Doing so keeps you alone in your suffering, and deprives you of the relief you might feel if you were to share with a close friend or loved one. Additionally, your critic tries to turn off the feelings of vulnerability by launching loud and vicious waves of self-attack. For example, imagine you meet a woman. You have a great connection with her, and she gives you her number at the end of the evening. You are excited about seeing her again and you look forward to setting up a date. But she does not respond to your phone calls or texts, and you have no idea why.

The natural response to this, especially if you were really excited about her, is to feel sad, disappointed, and frustrated. You might even feel some fear about the reality that you cannot control how other people act, yet are vulnerable to how they treat and respond to you. This is a fact of life. It is part of putting yourself out there. At times, you will get hurt. It is inevitable. These are all very authentic, tender, and vulnerable feelings.

Instead of staying with these feelings and letting them move through you, your critic launches a tirade against you.

What is wrong with you? You came off too needy! Of course she doesn't want to be with you! Who would?

Instead of feeling vulnerable, now you feel anxious and inadequate. As uncomfortable as these feelings are, they are a great distraction from the underlying feelings of vulnerability, which the critic *hates*.

This misguided approach is especially painful because when we feel afraid, nervous, worried, or vulnerable, the *last* thing we need is to be attacked. What we most need in these instances are words of kindness, love, support, and encouragement. We need to soothe that frightened, vulnerable part of ourselves until it is relaxed and calm.

FOUR STEPS TO SELF-COMPASSION

Step 1—Stop, breathe, & pay attention

The first part of cultivating a more compassionate and kind attitude towards ourselves is to recognize when we are in the cycle of self-criticism. We can be in this cycle for a long time before we even recognize it. Strong feelings of fear, anger, or self-loathing may indicate that we are in the cycle of self-criticism.

Once you notice you are in the cycle, the first thing to do is to stop what you are doing and breathe. Do not check your email, send a text message, or turn on some loud music. See if you can take a moment to pause and check in with your body. Can you feel your breath going in and out of your lungs?

Before you try to figure out what you are thinking or what you are feeling, just continue to breathe. It can be helpful to take three full, conscious breaths, paying close attention to the pauses in between your inhale and exhale. All the negative, spiraling thoughts will be waiting for you when you are ready to re-engage with them. For the time being, just focus on your breath to break the cycle and the circuit. As you are taking these breaths, guide your focus and pay attention to what is happening inside your body. Ask yourself:

- What's happening right now?
- What am I feeling?
- What am I thinking?
- What's going on in my body?
- How does my breath feel? Is it tight and constricted? Is it hard to take air in?
- Is my mind racing?
- Am I feeling scared?
- Am I worried that people aren't going to like me?
- What is *really* happening?

Step 2—Acknowledge suffering

The second step is to acknowledge the suffering that you are experiencing. Here are some examples of emotional suffering you might be dealing with in the moment:

- Fear
- Anger
- Pain
- Dislike
- Aversion
- Sadness
- Pessimism
- Despair
- Discouragement
- Hopelessness

Whatever it is, it is suffering—and it is uncomfortable. Often when we start to challenge our critic, we try to talk ourselves out of what we are feeling.

I shouldn't be feeling this way. Clearly if I just saw it differently, then I would feel better.

These thoughts can be just another source of self-attack.

I did not do a good enough job of challenging my critic. There's something wrong with me.

The key here is to simply acknowledge that you are experiencing painful feelings, and that you are suffering. This is a powerful part of creating compassion, because compassion occurs when you acknowledge suffering and have a desire to help the person who is struggling. In this case, the person is you.

Step 3—Empathize

Empathy is simply listening to and understanding the feelings of someone else. Have you ever shared something with someone, and felt much more relaxed and peaceful afterwards? This often is the result of being heard, understood, and witnessed in your struggle. This is empathy, and it is something we readily give to others.

The third step of creating self-compassion is learning how to give this kind of empathy to yourself. Instead of trying to talk yourself out of your feelings, or criticizing yourself for having the feelings, you can empathize with yourself. *Yes, it is really uncomfortable for me to go talk with those people. I am feeling really scared right now. Whew, this is tough. A lot of people feel this way.*

The attitude behind empathy for yourself is that all of your feelings matter, and they are all acceptable. A powerful way to capture this is by using the phrase "of course."

Of course I'm feeling anxious. I really want these people to like me. I don't have very many friends, and I haven't had that many friends. I want this to work out.

Of course I'm feeling angry and upset. This person said she was going to spend time with me, and now she doesn't want to. In fact, she wants to break up. Of course I'm feeling angry.

Of course I'm feeling sad. Anyone else in this situation would be feeling this way too.

Sometimes when we attack ourselves, we feel like we are the only ones suffering in a particular way. This can lead to feelings of personal inadequacy and loneliness, which can exacerbate an already overwhelming situation. We start to believe that we are the *only* people who feel social anxiety, and that everyone else has *no* problems with confidence.

In reality, many people struggle with this. Literally *millions* of people have social anxiety, and struggle with it intensely—perhaps more intensely than you do. Realizing you are not alone in your suffering is a big part of having self-empathy. Instead of seeing your anxiety as evidence of personal failure or inadequacy, you can start to see it as an inevitable part of being human. Perhaps fear, anxiety, anger, and other kinds of suffering are just part of being a person on this planet, and there is nothing wrong with you for feeling those emotions.

Step—Soothing yourself

Soothing yourself involves thinking and saying kind, compassionate, patient, loving, and supportive things to yourself. Start by placing your hand on your chest, just over your heart. This physical contact can be incredibly soothing, something a mother might do for her young child. Imagine a mother soothing an upset child. What would a good mother do in this situation? What would she say?

Darling, it's okay. You're okay sweetie. I know it's hard. You're doing okay.

Saying these kinds of phrases in your own mind or out loud can dramatically help you sooth yourself. There is something particularly powerful about terms of endearment, especially those that your parents or relatives used when you were young.

When I was young, my dad used to call me "buddy." When I am using this technique, I will say something like this to myself:

Hey buddy, you're doing okay. You're doing the best you can, Aziz. You're okay.

The exact words are less important than the soothing, calming, supportive tone you use with yourself. It is through this tone that you offer yourself the love and compassion you need in the moment. In addition to the tone, speaking the words out loud tends to increase their effect.

Thich Nhat Hanh, a world-renowned author, poet and teacher, captures this idea beautifully when he guides people through their suffering. He encourages them to place a hand on their heart and say the following:

My darling, I care about your suffering.

It is a statement of incredible validation, acknowledgement, and kindness, and stands in stark contrast to the negative, critical ways we might typically react to our suffering:

You're feeling this way again! What is wrong with you?

One final way to soothe yourself is to imagine what you would tell a friend in a similar situation. Imagine you wanted to ask someone out for a while, and you finally mustered the courage to try. When you did, she thanked you and said she wasn't interested. Afterwards, you began criticizing yourself:

I'm not attractive. I'm stupid. I'm awkward. I was too nervous.

Let's say a friend came to you and said the exact same thing:

"I tried to ask a girl out and she didn't want anything to do with me."

What would you say to him? You wouldn't say, "That makes sense. You are stupid, anxious and awkward," especially if you want to remain friends. Most likely, you would provide some sort of encouragement or support:

"Man, that sucks. You're actually a really good guy. Sure, not everyone is going to be interested, but there are plenty out there who are going to see your value and want to go out with you."

What would you offer a friend? Encouragement? Support?

What would you say? How could you treat yourself in a similar way? What could you say to yourself when you experience a failure or setback?

COMPASSIONATE LETTER WRITING

For many of us, speaking to ourselves in a self-soothing and compassionate manner is a little unusual, if not completely foreign. Doing so can feel silly or awkward, and the words might be hard to find. One way to increase your ability to speak to yourself kindly and caringly is to practice compassionate letter writing. This process involves writing a letter addressed to yourself that is full of supportive and compassionate statements. You can highlight the challenges you are facing in your life, then provide yourself with the deep support and encouragement that would benefit you.

The letter does not have to be elaborate or in-depth. It can simply highlight some of the challenges you faced that day. For example, let's say earlier at work, you went to the break room to get some water. A few people were standing around talking, and you did not know how to join or engage with them. You quietly got your water, feeling awkward during the silence, and quickly left the room. Afterwards you felt discouraged, embarrassed, and anxious.

While this ordinarily would be great fuel for the critic, imagine that you are practicing compassionate letter writing each night before you go to bed. In this case, you would sit down and write a brief letter addressed to yourself. For example:

Dear Aziz,

I'm sorry about the break room today. That was tough, wasn't it? The break rooms are the worst because there's this pressure to say something. I know it's something that you've been dealing with for a while and you're feeling discouraged about it.

I think you are doing a great job of addressing this though. You are reading this book and you are becoming more aware of yourself. You are also taking risks in a lot of other areas. This situation just happens to be particularly challenging. I'm sorry that it's difficult for you. I trust that you will learn how to be more comfortable in the future. And even if you don't, I still love you! You are a good person, and of course you're anxious in that situation. You are okay as you are.

OPTIMAL SELF-COACHING

In previous sections, you learned how to challenge your critic and soothe yourself. Both of these are recovery strategies— they help you respond to your critic's attacks. While that is an essential skill, we do not want to repair ourselves after each attack just to keep getting re-injured. We want to develop a strong, positive forward front so that we are actively encouraging and supporting ourselves, rather than just responding to continual internal threats.

In a sense, you want to consciously start your own propaganda campaign in a positive direction. This involves regularly giving yourself messages that will enhance your sense of well-being, and give you strength and courage to face life's inevitable challenges. A great way to understand this process is to imagine a helpful, effective, positive coach. This can be one from a team you played on, a team you like to watch, or even an entirely made up coach if you are not into sports. All of us have an internal coach that can help guide us through the challenges in our lives. The question is, what kind of coach are you going to create?

SUPPORT, ENCOURAGEMENT, PRAISE

What do positive coaches do? They support, encourage, and praise their players for doing well. They notice the positive things, and then highlight them to the players. They let them know when they have done something particularly well, which inspires them to keep doing that in the future. Most importantly, they believe in their players. They hold them accountable and encourage them to be their best. That is exactly what we can do when we become our own positive coaches.

One way to coach yourself is to consciously practice giving yourself support, encouragement, and praise—S.E.P.—frequently throughout the day. The self-critical propaganda campaign is running on multiple fronts throughout the day and night. For the S.E.P. campaign to take hold, we must actively remind ourselves about what we are doing well throughout the day. When we offer ourselves support when we need it—when we are struggling with something, or we are having a hard time—we can say out loud, "Hey, this is tough. This is a hard thing you're going through, but you are going to get through it. I believe in you and you can do this. You have a tremendous amount of courage and ability. I know you can handle this."

Notice how these statements include support for what is difficult, encouragement to keep going, and praise for what is good in you. The key with this practice is frequency and repetition. It is important to regularly catch yourself doing things well. One way to enhance this is to pick a number, such as 10. Commit for the day to notice and acknowledge 10 things that you did well or that are going well in a given day. They can be very simple, small things. The key is not to count only significant events, but to count many small events with a high frequency.

For example, let's say you have an alarm set, and you get up right when the alarm goes off. You offer yourself some encouragement or praise: *Well done, nice job.* You can say this in your mind, or if no one is around, you can say it out loud. Saying it out loud can make it more impactful because you are saying it and hearing it at the same time. Remember, the more multifaceted the propaganda campaign is, the more effective it will be.

Later that morning, perhaps during breakfast, you choose to resist sugary cereal, and instead eat a bowl of oatmeal. This is another great opportunity for praise. A little later it is time to go to work, and you are going to be late. Perhaps you feel anxious, and a worrisome thought enters your mind:

Oh my god, it's going to be terrible when I walk into that meeting. Everyone is going to look at me. I am so bad with time, what the hell is wrong with me? I'm always late to everything.

In this situation, you can offer yourself support:

Hey, this is tough. Being late is challenging, and I really don't like showing up when something's already started. I'm managing this well now, and I want to start taking care of myself by making sure I leave on time.

In order to become your own optimal coach, aim for 10 instances of support, encouragement and praise per day. This is especially important when you face a challenge that tends to trigger your critic.

Objection 1—That sounds lame

One common objection to being our own optimal coach is that it sounds a little ridiculous to talk to ourselves this way.

ShyQuote:
It sounds like I'm a dramatic cheerleader pumping myself up or something. It feels phony and forced.

I agree that saying many positive things per day to ourselves does feel a little cheesy and has a bit of a cheerleader ring to it. My question to you is, what is the quality of your life right now? If you are feeling peaceful, excited, or optimistic, it is probably directly related to the messages you give yourself on a daily basis. If you are feeling anxious, stuck, and pessimistic about your future, what kind of messages do you give and receive on a daily basis? On an hourly basis?

Simply put, the current messages that you give yourself—either out loud or just in your own mind—determine the quality of your life. How do statements such as the following impact you as you read them?

- That was stupid.
- That wasn't good enough.
- What the hell is wrong with you?
- You look like a fool.

Imagine hearing those messages in your own mind dozens of times per day. Is it worth it to try something a little cheesy if it will help you feel better? If we do not replace that critical propaganda campaign with a more effective one, then we are guaranteed to get the same negative feelings in a number of situations. When you talk with yourself in a positive way, you consciously take control of the process, and begin influencing your thoughts, actions and emotions in positive ways.

Objection 2—Raging egomaniac
The second objection to offering this type of personal support, encouragement, and praise is the fear of being an egomaniac:

Won't I be some egotistical blowhard if I am telling myself I'm great all the time?

Notice how this fear is very similar to the fears we have about giving ourselves compassion and acknowledging and owning our strengths. Both reflect a hypersensitivity to being egotistical or arrogant. The same response applies here. The more you support, encourage, and praise yourself—the more you begin seeing your strengths and what is good about you—the better you are going to feel about yourself. And the better you feel about yourself, the more you are able to connect with, support, and ultimately love others.

While you fear that you will be egotistical and people will not like you, the truth is that people will be drawn to you. There will be a magnetism about you that comes from you being truly comfortable in your own skin. This comfort draws others to you and can help them learn to be more comfortable with themselves as well.

Eight

TAKE BOLD ACTION

"Be daring, be different, be impractical, be anything that will assert integrity of purpose and imaginative vision against the play-it-safers, the creatures of the commonplace, the slaves of the ordinary."
~ *Cecil Beaton*

The first two components of the solution to social anxiety can be seen as the internal foundation of social confidence. Knowing who you are and having a strong sense of yourself can help you break free from the judgments—and the perceived judgments—of others. When you can be on your own side, manage your critic, and treat yourself with compassion, you are more prepared to weather the inevitable rejections and setbacks in life. This second component—accepting yourself fully—involves looking at areas where you tend to be harsh or rejecting towards yourself, and over time developing a deeper practice of loving and accepting who you are. This paves the way for you to truly receive love from others and to trust that people will like you for who you are.

The third component is to take bold action. The idea that you are not good enough and that people will not like you is something that has been ingrained into your mind over many years. You have hundreds of experiences that you can call up as evidence of the fact that people will not like you, and that things will not turn out well.

These ideas are incredibly convincing. They compel us to hesitate, to shy away, and to avoid the situations and people we find frightening. This sets up a reinforcing cycle where we avoid reaching out, do not get good responses from others as a result, and then gain further evidence that we are not worthy.

In order to truly overcome your social anxiety at a deep, gut level, you must *repeatedly* take bold action. It is only through trying something new, and with a different perspective, that you learn to see the world and the people around you in a different light.

DO WHAT SCARES YOU

YOUR INNER NEWTON

To better understand this process, imagine a curious, bright scientist who wants to discover the nature of gravity. What would he do? Most likely, he would develop some ideas or hypotheses, then go test them out with experiments. He would repeatedly conduct these experiments until he felt like he had a good understanding of gravity.

Just like a curious scientist, you have a hypothesis. For example, one hypothesis might be as follows:

If I start a conversation with an attractive stranger at a coffee shop, she will think I'm a weirdo and be disturbed or annoyed.

This is a great hypothesis and one worth testing. When scientists set up an experiment, they also create an alternative hypothesis, which is the opposite of the one they are testing. In this case, it would be:

If I start a conversation with an attractive stranger at a coffee shop, she will <u>NOT</u> think I'm a weirdo and be disturbed or annoyed.

This "null hypothesis," as scientists call it, simply describes the possibility that your hypothesis might not be correct. For example, your null hypothesis would be true if the other person felt neutral, liked you a little, or became your best friend or lover.

If you can view the process of taking bold action as that of a scientist exploring the nature of human interaction through many social experiments, you can take some of the charge out of the results you get. If the scientist runs a gravity experiment with an egg and he gets a result he was not expecting (the egg splats on the floor), would he viciously berate himself, conclude he is a fool, and feel embarrassed? Or would he pause, ponder, and try to understand what had occurred, and ask himself, "Why did the egg fall that way?" After questioning the outcome, perhaps he would simply run a few more experiments to find out what is going on.

You can approach taking bold action in the exact same way. Your experiments will give you information about how you and others operate. Over time, you will learn more and more about how to connect with others, and eventually see that no matter who you are, there are many people out there who want to be your friend, your lover, or your life partner.

WILLINGNESS

Being willing is the point where some people balk. I have seen this time and again when working with individuals and groups. People ask, "Do I really *have* to do this? Isn't there a different way? Can't I just read about it a little more and overcome it that way?" Or, my personal favorite, "What are you going to *make* me do?"

I often smile at this point, mainly because I get it. I have been in the exact same position. I avoided dating and relationships for most of my high school and college years for this exact reason. Of course we avoid. Doing the opposite is so damned uncomfortable!

I spent years thinking I needed to read and think about it a little more, to wait a little longer until I had it all figured out. I read several books on the subject and thought they were full of great ideas.

Perhaps reading just a bit more would help me make the changes I wanted. The truth is, reading more will not help you.

Insight and understanding are essential first steps, and they can help you learn new ways to see yourself and your situation. But in order to change on a deep level, you must at some point take action. You must take action again and again. It is not a one-time thing. It is a process of repeatedly trying things over time.

It is perfectly natural and reasonable to feel anxious or reluctant to try new things. After all, this is the nature of fear—we want to avoid doing the thing we are afraid of at all costs. That is part of being human. However, in order to overcome a fear, we must be willing to move towards it, even if we are deeply afraid. Would you be willing to try something that is uncomfortable or frightening if you knew that it could change your life forever? What if doing so would make it easier for you to walk into a room full of new people and enjoy yourself? What would it be worth to you if you could leave a dinner party and feel excited and happy about the connections you made, and not criticize yourself?

Would facing your fear be worth it if you were able to go somewhere and strike up conversations with people you found interesting, or to whom you were attracted? What if you could approach a woman in order get to know her, and find out if she was available and interested in *you?*

If you want these things, and if they are worth it to you, then you must be willing to give it a shot. Don't worry—we will start slowly. Over time, you'll build up the ability to take bold action. All you need right now is willingness.

FEAR HIERARCHY

When learning to take bold action, it is helpful to gain an understanding of what exactly frightens us. Once we have a map of our fears, we are more equipped to approach them systematically. In behavioral psychology, this map is referred to as a *fear hierarchy*, and ranks our fears from most frightening to least frightening. Each one is paired with a number, to give you a sense of how scary it is.

The process of overcoming your fears through bold action involves pushing yourself slightly outside of your comfort zone. You begin by repeatedly doing the actions that are lower down on your hierarchy (numbers 1-4), eventually working your way up towards the top. This approach allows you to learn how to manage your anxiety and to gain confidence along the way. It is done at an appropriate pace and never forced, which is why it is called *gradual exposure*.

Creating Your Fear Hierarchy

Before creating your fear hierarchy, you must determine what areas of your life tend to cause anxiety, social fear, and self-criticism. Take a moment to brainstorm some things you have been afraid to do in the past. These might be things you completely avoid and seem totally impossible for you now.

Do you remember ranking your fears in the first chapter? Below is an extended list of fears to rank. For each scenario, take a moment to imagine what it would be like to be in that situation, and then rank how fearful it would be.

When ranking these items it is important to note how much you tend to avoid the scenario. When I was working with Jason, a young man who was good looking and affable but did not quite know it yet, I noticed he was marking items much lower than I expected. This brief transcript from our session will help you learn how avoidance plays a part in his rankings:

> Aziz: What about approaching an attractive woman to start a conversation?
>
> Jason: I'm not sure—maybe a four or five.
>
> Aziz: Four or five? It seems like that situation is not particularly nerve wracking for you then.
>
> Jason: No, not really.
>
> Aziz: How often do you do something like that?
>
> Jason: (shaking his head) No, I would never *do* something like that.
>
> Aziz: What if you imagine doing something like that right now? How anxious would you be if in a moment we went outside and found two attractive women to approach and start a conversation? How anxious would you be?
>
> Jason: (shaking his head the whole time) Wow, I don't know. I would never do something like that. A hundred!

This exchange shows how we tend to be less scared of situations we find very frightening because we are certain that we will avoid them. When assigning each item a number, be sure to rank it based upon how frightened you would be if you were actually in that situation.

Try completing this exercise without looking back to your rankings from the first chapter. After completing it, you can go back if you like to compare your answers from earlier. You might be surprised to see that some of your numbers have gone down, simply from reading the chapters in between.

Situation	Fear (1-10)
Going to a party or social gathering where you know most people	
Going to a party where you know almost no one	
Giving a prepared presentation to a group of people	
Speaking spontaneously in a front of a group of people	
Eating alone in public	
Going to the movie theater alone	
Calling someone you don't know very well	
Approaching an attractive stranger to start a conversation	
Approaching several attractive strangers to start a conversation	
Meeting someone new	

Speaking up in a group of people	
Dancing while sober	
Having a conversation with someone you don't know very well	
Urinating in a public bathroom	
Being the center of attention	
Disagreeing with someone you don't know very well	
Flirting with someone you find attractive	
Letting someone know you are interested in them sexually	
Complimenting a stranger	
Asking someone you find attractive out for a date	
Directly expressing anger to the person you are upset with	
Chatting with the cashier at a supermarket	

Making eye contact with a stranger on the street	
Talking with an elderly person out in public (bus stop, store, etc.)	
Asking a store clerk for help with something	
Returning an item to a store	
Talking with someone you know very well	

To create your fear hierarchy, simply write down one or two items for each level. You do not need to worry about the lowest numbers (one and two), since those situations produce very little anxiety. Make sure each number between three and ten has at least one item in it. See below for an example of Jason's hierarchy:

Level	Feared Situation
10	Approaching an attractive stranger to start a conversation. Letting someone know I am interested in them sexually. Asking someone I find attractive out for a date.
9	Speaking spontaneously in front of a group of people. Dancing while sober. Flirting with someone I find attractive.
8	Going to a party where I know almost no one there. Being the center of attention.

7	Giving a prepared presentation. Meeting someone new. Disagreeing with someone I don't know very well.
6	Going to a party where I know most people there. Having a conversation with someone I don't know very well.
5	Urinating in a public bathroom. Eating alone in public. Making eye contact with a stranger on the street.
4	Going to a movie theater alone. Chatting with the cashier at a supermarket.
3	Talking with an elderly person out in public. Asking a store clerk for help with something.

Take a moment now to create your own fear hierarchy. You can use the items that you ranked in the list above, and you can add other specific situations to your hierarchy. Be sure to have at least one item for each level, and preferably more.

Level	Feared Situation
10	
9	
8	
7	
6	
5	
4	
3	

Changing your relationship with fear

Now that you have a fear hierarchy, what do you do with it? The most common question I get once we have constructed a hierarchy is, "What are you going to make me do?"

In the case of this book, I am not going to make you do anything. The "no pain, no gain" philosophy does not work for overcoming shyness. If we demand too much of ourselves and push ourselves forward relentlessly, it does not produce better or faster results. The key to using your fear hierarchy as a transformational tool is to allow it to help you *fundamentally change the way you deal with fear*. This includes changing the way you see, respond to, and approach fear.

For most of us, fear means flee. If something is scary, we want to avoid it. This is a very deeply ingrained pattern in all animals, and can be beneficial for survival. However, when we experience social anxiety, we perceive many things as potential threats, even things that cannot actually harm us—such as when someone disapproves of, judges, or dislikes us. When we are anxious, we see these outcomes as *terrible threats* we must avoid at all costs. In order to avoid, we flee, which leaves us with an ever-decreasing range of social options.

In order to take bold action towards overcoming social anxiety, we must shift our relationship with fear[7]. The first step is to realize that everyone feels fear. Even those of us who look very confident, or are able to speak in front of large groups with apparent ease, still experience fear. If you are growing, trying new things, learning and expanding yourself, then you are going to feel fear.

When I share this fact with people, some find it hard to believe. The reality is that some famous musicians and performers

---

7. Susan Jeffers' book, entitled *Feel The Fear And Do It Anyway* (New York: Random House, 1987) is a quick, powerful read that can help you dramatically change the way you see fear.

get stage fright, even after performing for many years. I have spent hundreds of hours speaking and facilitating discussions in front of large groups of people. Each time, about one day before the seminar or lecture, I start to get nervous, self-conscious, and increasingly self-critical. I have learned that I need to increase my practices of self-compassion, and make sure to take extra care of myself in the days leading up to a lecture. Once I get started, the fear subsides and I generally enjoy myself greatly. However, the fear and anticipation is there again before the next seminar.

When people step forward and put themselves out there, it's not a matter of how much fear they feel, but rather how willing they are to take action *in spite of the fear.*

Something powerful happens inside of us when we make the shift from avoidance to approach when it comes to fear. Your fear hierarchy is precisely designed to help you make this shift. Instead of viewing each item as a threat that demands your focus, time, and energy to avoid, what if you saw each item as an opportunity to face your fears?

When it comes to social fear, the only way out is through. You must break the cycle that says you are not good enough, that people will not like you, and that you are not worthy of love. And this means taking bold action—literally stepping *towards the thing* you fear. Only through repeatedly exposing ourselves to that which scares us can we learn, on a gut level, that our fears are often unfounded. People generally *do* like us, and when they do not, it is not the end of the world. We can handle it.

No amount of reading the above statement or thinking about it will produce a lasting result. The only way to change our anxiety on a deep level is to patiently and repeatedly expose ourselves to what scares us.

Using your fear hierarchy

Your hierarchy is your own customized road map to help you go from social fear to liberation. The process is simple to understand, yet difficult to carry out. To that end, this process can be greatly accelerated and made more enjoyable by finding a close friend or trusted companion to "buddy up" with. If you work on your hierarchies together, the process will be much more enjoyable.

The key to the hierarchy is to begin in the lower ranges, where the situations are much less anxiety provoking. During the course of the week, set a goal for yourself to complete one or several items from the lowest level on your hierarchy, starting with level three. Items in this range should be only mildly anxiety-provoking, and are things that you might not enjoy, but that you can get yourself to do without too much fear or angst.

Each week, set a new goal for yourself to complete another item from slightly higher on the hierarchy, moving up to the items in level four, then five, and so on. When you reach an item that is particularly anxiety provoking, be sure to repeat it *many times* over the course of several weeks.

For example, if you are uncomfortable making eye contact with a stranger on the street, then you can take some time to walk down a busy street with many pedestrians, purposefully holding eye contact with as many people as you can. You can also smile and greet them if you like. This task, dubbed *Smile and Hello*[8] practice by David Burns, can help you repeatedly practice making eye contact with a stranger.

The goal is to regularly practice something that is slightly out of your comfort zone. Your comfort zone is the range of activities you do that produce no anxiety whatsoever. When

---

8. David Burns describes this process and many other useful techniques to help overcome social anxiety in his book *Intimate Connections* (New York: Penguin Group, 1985).

attempting to increase your social confidence, it is necessary to systematically push beyond the limits of your comfort zone.

For some, going to an extreme and flooding themselves with what scares them is efficient and effective. For most, however, the most effective route is to steadily and patiently push yourself to do something just slightly beyond what you feel comfortable doing. The goal is to feel anxiety, but not to be overwhelmed by the feelings.

As you work your way up the hierarchy, you might notice three very interesting things about how fear works. First, you may start to see that much of the fear you feel occurs *before* you engage in the activity. You will also see that if you stay in the frightening situation long enough, your fear level will eventually begin to decrease. The intense spike of fear that you feel before you take the risk is unsustainable. Your body will naturally calm down after about 10 or 15 minutes, even if you are still in the situation.

Second, you will see that once you have completed an item on the list many times, your fear of that situation decreases. The first time you start a conversation with a stranger, it might be incredibly nerve wracking. However, after the 30th time, it might prompt minimal anxiety, and may even be enjoyable.

A third realization you might have is that some of the higher levels start to become less scary *even before you do them.* I will not go into too much detail here about why that is, because I prefer for you to experience this phenomenon for yourself as you work through your hierarchy.

The most important thing to remember is that the more you move towards what scares you, and the more you take bold action, the more powerful you become. You will be less influenced by your fear, and more able to do what you truly want in life, even if you are frightened as you do it. Best of all, the things that scare you will become less frightening.

Imaginal exposure

When it comes to the more intimidating numbers on your hierarchy (seven and above), it can be helpful to practice before you engage in the activity. One powerful way to practice from the comfort of your own home is through what is referred to as *imaginal exposure*. This involves vividly creating the scene in your mind before you engage in the activity. Your body responds to vivid imagery and your imagination almost as potently as if you were actually in the scenario.

For example, let's say you have a fear of eating alone at a restaurant. You listed this as a seven on your hierarchy, and it is something you routinely avoid. As you progress up your hierarchy, you can choose to go out for a nice meal by yourself as a social experiment. In the meantime, however, you can use imaginal exposure to work through some of your fears. The key for this exposure, as with any, is to make sure that you actually feel the anxiety as you are going through it. As you read the section below, allow yourself to imagine the scene in detail:

You are arriving at an upscale restaurant in your city. You have decided to take yourself out for a nice meal for no reason other than because you deserve it. As you walk into the restaurant, the hostess asks you how many are in your party. See yourself smiling and calmly telling her the table is for one this evening. Notice how you feel as you say this to her, if there is any fear or embarrassment in your body. Taking a deep breath in, you walk towards your table and sit down, scooting your chair up to the white tablecloth.

Allow yourself to see the course of the entire evening—the server coming to take your drink order, food order, and eventually to deliver your food. Imagine seeing the people in tables around you. Now imagine looking at them and seeing them as they are. Notice that, at certain points during the meal, other people look at you. Notice if your mind fears they are judging you, making conclusions about you, or pitying you. See yourself smiling and breathing, and being able to handle whatever responses you get from the strangers around you.

Imagine finishing the last bite of an outstandingly delicious meal, pushing your plate forward, and leaning back in your chair with a sigh of satiated delight. The best part of all was that you realized that you can treat yourself to a nice meal any time you want.

What did you experience reading through the imaginal exposure exercise? Did it produce anxiety or fear in you? If so, perfect! The goal of this type of exposure is to get you to feel the discomfort you might feel in the moment. Each time you experience that discomfort and do not flee or avoid it, you strengthen your ability to take bold action.

THE BACKLASH

One important point to realize as you embark on this transformational journey of moving *towards* what scares you, is that there might be some turbulence along the way. As author and motivational speaker Les Brown says, when you are ascending to a new altitude, it can get bumpy on the way up before it levels out[9]. Sometimes, when you push yourself to the ledge and take a leap, there can be a feeling of elation. You might feel incredibly liberated talking with that stranger, or asking that person out for a date.

After this period of elation, however, there is often something that I refer to as "The Backlash." This is your inner critic, who was temporarily pushed aside long enough for you to

---

9.   Les Brown is an incredibly inspiring speaker who strongly encourages people to pursue their dreams with passion and persistence. His book *It's Not Over Until You Win* (New York: Fireside, 1997) contains many of his core teachings. In addition, a YouTube search will provide you with access to dozens of full-length video recordings of his lectures.

take bold action, trying to regain control. Remember, your critic does not want you to take risks, to put yourself out there, or to face rejection. It is terrified that you will experience more pain because people might not like or approve of you. By taking bold action, you are going against the inner critic's propaganda campaign, and its primary response is to turn the volume up.

After you have spoken up for yourself, blurted out something you were curious about, given a presentation, eaten alone at a restaurant, or done any other item on your hierarchy, you might be subject to the backlash. This includes an intense feeling of shame, discomfort, embarrassment, humiliation, fear of disapproval, and general self-loathing. This backlash can be so intense that people think they have made a mistake. *This approach doesn't work at all. I feel **worse** than before I started.*

This is exactly what your internal critic wants you to think. If it can create enough self-doubt and questioning, then you are one step closer to going back to your life where the critic had you under its complete control. At this point your critic is terrified that you are going to adopt a lifestyle that involves taking healthy risks, facing your fears, and going towards what you want most despite potential failure or rejection. This is unbearable to your critic. It will do what it can to cause you to give up, to stop taking risks, and to go back to playing small.

In order to overcome social anxiety, and to truly liberate yourself to talk with strangers, make friends, and create deep and satisfying romantic relationships, you must persevere through each backlash and try again. You can use your skills of self-acceptance and self-compassion to help you through the backlash periods. Over time the backlashes become less frequent, and don't last as long. More importantly, you will become skilled at identifying them and realize they are just an inevitable part of this process.

FACING REJECTION

The basic assumption of social anxiety makes us particularly vulnerable to rejection. We believe that *because I am not good enough, people will reject me*. When we walk around carrying this belief, we are assuming people will reject us, and we are terrified of this happening because it proves our worst fears. We can then blow things up in our minds and conclude that everyone will reject us for the rest of our lives.

This section is about helping you change the way you relate to rejection, just like the last section helped you change the way you relate to fear.

REFRAMING REJECTION

No matter who you are, rejection is inevitable. Rejection is even more likely as you start to pursue goals and dreams that really matter to you. When you take an active stance towards your life, when you get out of the bleachers and onto the field, rejection can become a regular occurrence. And we do not like rejection. It feels painful, uncomfortable, and embarrassing. We tend to conclude that it means something bad about us, or that we did something terribly wrong.

In response to rejection, we often think: *If only I were smarter, quicker, or somehow better, then I could have prevented this rejection*. This mindset reveals that we assume that we should never be rejected. It also reveals that when we are rejected, we tend to take it personally and conclude that it means we are in some way inadequate. Below we will discuss three powerful ways to reframe rejection and change the way you relate to this inevitable part of life.

Stop personalizing

When we get rejected, it can be very difficult not to take it personally. Before we even realize what we are doing, we can feel hollow inside and worth barely more than the dirt we stand on. *Personalizing* is a term used to describe taking too much personal responsibility for a situation that involves multiple people and multiple elements. It occurs when we conclude that the rejection was totally our fault and it reflects our personal inadequacy. Somewhere in all of our minds we have learned this formula:

REJECTION = INADEQUATE

If someone rejects me, it means I'm bad, not good enough, and not worthy. This process can happen rapidly and beneath our conscious awareness. We do not think about it too much, we simply feel it on a gut level. It is a full body emotion that can make breathing, standing, and looking people in the eye difficult.

One powerful way to break this instinctive habit of personalization is to explore what else rejection could mean by regularly asking ourselves this simple question:

What else could this mean?

If you start a conversation with someone, and they are not interested in continuing it with you, could it mean something much different than your negative interpretation?

Perhaps she prefers to be alone. Maybe you two are simply not a good fit. Maybe she is upset or hurt about something that has nothing to do with you, or she is just in a bad mood. Maybe *she* is shy and ends the conversation quickly because she is nervous and doesn't know what to say.

The main takeaway here is that rejection not only *could* mean something else, it most always *does*. The key is to first become aware of the fact that your *idea* of its meaning—that you are at fault, that you are a loser, that she simply doesn't like you—is not the truth. From there, you must seek alternative meanings that do not involve personalization and heavy self-criticism.

Staying with disappointment

It is painful when someone we are interested in doesn't want to go out with us, or when we don't get a job we want. These experiences are part of life, and demonstrate how vulnerable we are. Some of us deal with the disappointment by focusing on all the things we did wrong. This creates the illusion that if we just did everything perfectly, we would never have to experience these feelings. The truth is no matter who you are—no matter how good looking, how qualified, how desirable—you are not always going to get what you want. People and opportunities will pass you by, even when you try your best to go after them. Sadness, loss, frustration, and disappointment are normal, natural, and healthy.

Of course you are disappointed—that person, job, or goal really mattered to you! Give yourself the space to really feel the disappointment. Feel the sinking or heaviness in your chest or stomach. Feel the internal resistance to being rejected. Feel the sadness or tears behind your eyes.

The more you can simply feel the emotion without going into a story about why you were not good enough, the more quickly it will pass through you. This disappointment can serve to remind you how meaningful it is for you to meet a partner, or find your ideal job. It can also serve to strengthen and fuel you to pursue your dreams with a new passion and vigor.

Do not give up prematurely

For some, the first response to even a hint of rejection is to give up. As they approach the thing they want, they repeatedly tell themselves they are not good enough, and it will simply not work out anyway. This is a way of trying to manage feelings of disappointment, although it never really works. Rather, it causes people to use the first hint of rejection as a reason to stop, to say, "I knew I wasn't good enough. Why even try?" When you do this, you revert to the default interpretation of rejection—*you are not good enough.*

Rejection does not mean you are inadequate. It simply means that right now, the answer is no. Nowhere is this more common than in the area of dating and relationships. When we are attracted to someone—*really* attracted to someone—what do we usually do about it? We see her sitting on the other side of the room, chatting with a stranger, and we admire her hair, face, mannerisms, and figure. What is the most common response? That's right—to do nothing! Most often we talk ourselves out of it, assuming she would not want to talk with us anyway, she already has a boyfriend, she's out of our league, etc.

On the off chance that you do go speak with her, you are already so poised for rejection, that you take the first sideways glance or awkward pause in the conversation as undeniable proof that she thinks you are an unworthy loser. Instead of assuming disapproval and hastily throwing in the towel, is it possible to view any sort of rejection as a temporary setback? What if you approached someone and the person did not seem particularly engaged in the conversation with you? Is that reason enough to never try again?

Simon, a middle-aged man who had not been in a relationship since his divorce four years ago told me that it would take him years to start a relationship with someone new. When I asked him why, he replied that if a woman rejected him, it would take him three months before he could try again.

Three months?" I exclaimed. "That is a long time to recover from a rejection."

"If that," he said with a stern look on his face. "Maybe six."

"Who determines how long it will take before you can try again?"

As we continued to talk, he realized that there was no official "refresh rate" for overcoming rejection. The faster he could move on from a no, the more quickly he could find someone who would be excited to date him.

When we face rejection, it can be a poignant time to tap into our desire, motivation, drive, and passion to pursue what we most want.

- *Why do I want this?*
- *Why does it matter to me?*
- *Am I willing to do whatever it takes to get there?*

From this place, you are primed to try again. You can ask more questions, express curiosity, and even tell her what is on your mind.

Of course, if you try again and receive a clear *no,* then you can move on to another person, another job, another opportunity. Does this mean you are a loser for not getting what you wanted here? Or does it show you have the tenacity and spirit to try for something that you truly want?

REJECTION PRACTICE

By this point it has become clear that we avoid rejection because it often leads to painful feelings of inadequacy. Like most painful things, our natural response is to shy away from coming into contact with them. In addition to learning to reframe rejection, learning to engage in *rejection practice* is one of the most powerful ways of overcoming your fears.

Imagine for a moment that you had a terrible phobia of spiders. When I was a child I absolutely hated spiders. I had nightmares that they were crawling in my bed. Imagine you had a fear like this that persisted past childhood, and lasted to the present.

Worse still, your fear is so great that you still have panic attacks whenever you go somewhere a spider *might* be.

If you decide one day you are sick of your fear, and are ready to do something about it, you might see a psychologist who will guide you through an exposure treatment for spider phobia. This involves progressively exposing yourself to contact with an actual spider. You would not start immediately with direct contact, of course, because it would be too overwhelming. Instead, you would start by talking about spiders. Then you might take some time to imagine a spider, or look at an image of a spider. Eventually, you would progress to being in the same room as a spider in a cage, such as at a pet shop. The final stage of treatment would involve you having the spider on your arm at the pet shop. The essence of exposure is to directly experience the thing you are afraid of most.

The same holds true for social anxiety—which we can also call *social phobia*, or *social fear*. In this case, you're afraid that others will judge, ridicule, dislike, or reject you. As you work your way up your fear hierarchy, you will expose yourself to greater levels of judgment and rejection. It's important to realize that the purpose of completing these activities is not to succeed without any negative responses or rejections, but to actually *experience rejection*.

Avoiding while exposing

Lisa had completed her fear hierarchy and was eager, anxious, excited, and hesitant all at the same time to start taking bold action. An item she felt ready to try involved walking up to a stranger she did not know and asking them if they knew of a good restaurant nearby. She had been deathly afraid of strangers for as long as she could remember, and we had designed this social experiment to test how friendly (or deadly) strangers really were.

The day of her experiment arrived, and she left for her lunch break a little early. She nervously walked the streets, looking for someone to ask. She saw a white-haired man in his early sixties and decided to take the plunge. She walked up to him and started a conversation.

Lisa: Um, excuse me.
Man: *(turning to look at her)* Huh? What?
Lisa: Hi there, sorry to bother you. Uh, do you know of, um, a good restaurant in the area? I'm looking for some lunch.
Man: Lunch? I have no idea about that.

With that, he turned and hastily walked off in the opposite direction. Lisa stared after him with her mouth hanging open. What had just happened?

"What was that all about?" she angrily asked me in her next session. "I thought these experiments were supposed to show me that people were nice and friendly. It just confirmed what I always knew about strangers. The experiment was a failure."

"It certainly doesn't sound pleasant," I agreed. "But, I actually think it was more of a success than it might seem. The goal with these experiments is not to *avoid* the rejection of a stranger. It is to experience the fear of approaching something that scares you, and then to experience the discomfort of the rejection if it happens."

"Oh God, that's terrible!" Lisa exclaimed. "I can't keep doing that."

"What happened after he walked away from you?" I asked.

"He, um, well, he just walked down the street. I stood there for a moment feeling mortified, then I scurried off in embarrassment."

"Did he yell at you? Did anyone around the area point and laugh or giggle?" I asked with curiosity.

"No." She said, crossing her arms.

"It sounds like you handled the rejection quite well. I'm sure it didn't feel good. In fact, I'm sure it felt terrible. But it is exactly the medicine you need to overcome your fear of it. The whole point of these experiments is to come face-to-face with your fear, to get rejected, and to realize that you are still standing. The ultimate point is to see that aside from what happens in our own minds, the actual harm or danger of rejection is often very minor."

A friend and teacher of mine, Dr. Matthew May, once told me that the way to get over rejection is to take many "rejection inoculations." Much like an inoculation, if you take regular, small doses of rejection over time, it does not make you sick when you experience it.

ASSUME APPROVAL

Another way to manage rejection is to interrupt the pattern of continually rejecting yourself in your own mind. When you are feeling anxious, you are most likely disqualifying yourself long before you ever open your mouth to speak. In other words, you are probably subconsciously assuming other people will not like you.

Imagine for a moment that you are in your favorite coffee shop. You are waiting to receive your drink and you look to your left and see a woman standing there, waiting for her drink as well. What a perfect opportunity to strike up a conversation. What happens next? In fact, what happens as you imagine this scenario? Do you get nervous just thinking about it? Does your heart beat faster? Do your palms become moist?

Most people in this scenario will pretend to be totally absorbed in that Starbucks CD rack, sneaking furtive glances at this compelling stranger. They think to themselves:
What do I say? I have nothing to talk about. She probably already has a boyfriend. She can see me looking at her. She probably thinks I'm a creep.

Then she finally gets her coffee and walks off and you breathe a sigh of relief.

Whew...

Only moments later you feel a pang of regret, which feels more like a sigh of dismay than relief. You may even start criticizing yourself for not being more outgoing. Self-attack aside, why didn't you talk with her?

While all the reasons that passed through your mind are part of the story, the underlying reason is that on some level *you assumed she would not like you,* and would therefore disapprove. Remember, when we feel socially anxious, we buy the idea that there is something wrong with us. If we believe this, it is only logical that we would expect disapproval and rejection.

Self-fulfilling prophecy

The problem with assuming disapproval is that we tend to perceive, and even actively create, what we expect to happen in our lives. If you are certain that someone is not going to like you, then when you speak with him, you will be paying closer attention to his subtle gestures and mannerisms. What did that sigh mean? Why did he look away before he answered me? Or, why didn't he smile when I made that joke? When the underlying assumption is disapproval, it's easy to see any scenario as proof that someone does not like you.

When we have a strong belief about something, we go even further than simply perceiving more evidence for it. We can go so far as to bring about the result we are expecting, in order to prove our belief to be true. In the scenario of meeting someone, if you are convinced they will reject you, how do you think you will engage them? Will you be warm, friendly, open, and vulnerable? Or might you be guarded, hesitant, quiet, and non-responsive? If you are expecting disapproval, it might be challenging to not act from a position of self-protection and guardedness.

The person you are speaking with will pick up on this and might start to feel self-conscious or uncomfortable. In fact, he might not be able to feel connected to you, and he might think you are disinterested in him, or in what he is saying. As a result, he might end the interaction hastily and go talk with someone else.

"Ah ha!" you might say. "I knew he wouldn't like me." All the while, your assumptions about the interaction actually created the outcome you feared. This is called a *self-fulfilling prophecy.*

How to assume approval

Assuming approval is a powerful antidote to the fear of rejection. It uses the principle of a self-fulfilling prophecy, but instead assumes that people *will* like you. Instead of assuming disapproval, dislike and rejection, you can assume approval, friendliness, and engagement. This technique requires asking yourself a question before you engage in a social interaction:

"How would I act if I knew beyond a shadow of a doubt that the people here loved me and found me delightful?"

Can you think of a friend or family member who you know loves you, and will be on your side no matter what? How do you behave around this person? What do you talk about? What jokes do you make? What are your bodily gestures like around this person?

Assuming approval involves taking all of these behaviors and attitudes, and consciously acting them out when you engage with people you do not know as well. In a way you are assuming friendship, as if you have known each other for years. What would this look like for you? Often it involves being more relaxed in your body, touching people on the shoulder or back, laughing out loud, making jokes, teasing, being playful, saying whatever comes to mind, asking questions about whatever you are curious about, and generally being your natural self.

Not only does this approach allow you to feel more relaxed when interacting with others, it actually brings about a more positive response from those around you. Your assumption of connection and approval puts people at ease and allows you to look past minor road bumps along the way. Your mind will be seeking information that confirms that they do in fact like you and think you are a great person, which will influence where you focus your attention.

THE FEARED FANTASY

As you are taking bold action in the world and approaching what you are afraid of, you will inevitably experience rejections. By this point, hopefully you are seeing that rejection is a natural part of life, and a necessary part of achieving success. There is no way to get what you truly want without experiencing rejections, setbacks, and failures along the way. While this fact might encourage us to keep pursuing our goals, it does not necessarily make the sting of rejection any less unpleasant. It can be very valuable to learn how to manage rejection and your fear of rejection, so that it does not stop you dead in your tracks.

One powerful way to work with your fear of rejection is to do an exercise called the *Feared Fantasy*. This is a technique that Dr. David Burns developed to use with clients during cognitive therapy.[10] Dr. Burns realized that the rejection his clients feared often revealed information about their own self-judgment. In order to prepare for rejection, he found it very empowering to have them practice responding to these imagined rejections, as if they were happening in the moment.

---

10. For more details about the Feared Fantasy technique, consult *Intimate Connections* by David Burns.

To use the Feared Fantasy approach, imagine a situation in which you are afraid of rejection—perhaps talking with that intriguing woman from the coffee shop example above. You might be paralyzed by the fear that she'll reject you, and all the other patrons will look up from their lattes and notice. In this case, you would pick the type of rejection you are the most afraid of, which might be an onlooker who sees you crash and burn and judges you heavily for it. Once you have identified the worst critic, you engage in a dialogue with that critic, as if it was a real person.

> Critic: Excuse me, did you just start a conversation up with that woman who walked out?

> Me: Why yes I did.

> Critic: Wow, that was pathetic. How embarrassing.

> Me: Oh, you saw that? Yeah, it certainly didn't go how I hoped it would.

> Critic: I'll say. That was pathetic. You are such a loser.

> Me: Wow, that's really harsh. You seem upset with me about this.

> Critic: No, I'm not upset. I'm just judging you for being so awkward.

> Me: Well, I'm proud of myself for giving it a shot, and it was a little awkward there for a moment. I think it's the only way I'll learn.

> Critic: Yeah right, you can't learn this.

Me: Really? I've heard that I can. Are you able to talk with a stranger at a coffee shop?

Critic: (scoffs) Of course. Anyone with half a brain can.

Me: Great! Do you have any pointers for me? I'm looking to improve.

Critic: No. I certainly do not. I don't think you can get better. You are just too much of a pathetic loser.

Me: Wow, you seem angry with me. Was that woman your girlfriend or something?

What did you notice about the exchange between you and this imaginary hostile critic? More often than not, when you engage with a worst-case scenario critic, you discover how unreasonable the critic can be. If someone were so harshly critical and unreasonable in real life, you might start to take them a little less seriously!

It can be incredibly helpful to do this exercise out loud with a friend, or by yourself in a journal. If doing it with a friend, you can let her know what you fear your critic would say, and then have her play the part of this imaginary critic. If she is as unreasonable and unrelenting as your critic, then both of you might be laughing before the exercise is through.

Below is an example of another feared fantasy from a client who was afraid to eat at a restaurant alone. We decided to do this exercise based upon what someone in the restaurant might say to her:

Critic: Are you eating a meal alone because you don't have any friends?

Me: Wow, what a forward thing to say. You seem awfully interested in what I'm doing over here. Since you asked though, I actually prefer to eat alone sometimes.

Critic: Yeah, well, I just think it's pathetic when I see some-one eating alone.

Me: Pathetic? That's a serious judgment. Sounds like you would never even consider eating alone.

Critic: Certainly not. I am popular and have lots of friends to eat with.

Me: *(Laughs)* With your tact, I can see why. I'm just kidding, you're alright.

～⌣⌣⌣⌣⌣～

The main point of this exercise is to imagine the worst things that an external critic might say to you. By dialoguing with this imaginary figure, you help yourself realize that you can handle whatever real-life criticism comes your way. Furthermore, you can start to see how much of your fear of criticism from the outside is simply your own inner critic projected onto others. This exercise can give you a window into the ways in which you criticize yourself, which will help you realize where you might need to develop self-acceptance and self-compassion.

A life without rejection

Even after acknowledging that rejection is an inevitable part of life and a necessary stepping stone on the way to success, and even after learning how to reframe rejection and manage painful feelings, actively embracing rejection can be difficult. One final way to better understand rejection is to take a moment to imagine a life *without* it.

Imagine for a moment that you were never rejected, never shot down, and never denied. No one ever told you no, disagreed with you, frowned, disapproved, or disliked you. Sounds pretty nice, doesn't it?

What would a life like that look like in reality? This is an important question. Right now, tens of thousands of people in the world are attempting to create a life without rejection. Unfortunately, in the world we live in, the only way to avoid rejection is to avoid taking risks. The only way to avoid hearing no is to never ask. To avoid being shot down, we have to avoid putting ourselves out there. In order to avoid being rejected, we must avoid engaging in life.

People that live lives without rejection are engaged in a habit of great avoidance.

- They avoid standing up for themselves.
- They avoid asking for what they deserve at work and in relationships.
- They avoid close friendships.
- They avoid confrontation.
- And sadly, they avoid love.

A life without rejection is a lonely life indeed.

The alternative is to step into life, to move towards what we want in spite of what we fear, to try again and again with an unreasonable refusal to quit. As Les Brown would say, the alternative is to take life on[11]. This involves getting off the sidelines, out of the bleachers and onto the field. This involves realizing that you might need to learn a few things and build some new skills. You might get knocked down, and you might even get a few bruises and cuts along the way. While at first this might not seem much better than being safe on the sidelines, after you have spent some time on the field you will never want to go back.

SPEAKING UP FOR YOURSELF

Taking bold action in the world not only involves where you choose to go and who you choose to interact with, but also includes *how* you communicate with the world around you. After years of avoidance and dodging rejection, many people with social anxiety have a way of being in the world that keeps them small, quiet, and under the radar. Many of them have felt as if others do not acknowledge them, or as if they are invisible.

Amir, a client I worked with to overcome his shyness, spent many years keeping a low profile. This helped him avoid being bullied in middle and high school. He carried this pattern forward and tended to keep to himself at work. He was a quiet, respectful hard worker. But he had no friends or acquaintances at work. He often joked that if he did not show up for a week no one would notice until they saw that his job duties were incomplete.

As we got to know each other, it became clear that one of his main motives for remaining small was that he did not want to be perceived as a threat to anyone. He believed that if he was

---

11. For a list of recommended Les Brown materials, see the Recommended Resources section at the end of the book.

noticeable and the center of attention, people would feel threatened by him. Other men would regard his eye contact and direct communication as aggressive and would fight back. Women would find those qualities forward and invasive and would harshly reject him. As a result of these beliefs, he decided to live his life by not being a *threat*. Once we discovered what his definition of threat was, I playfully encouraged him to start becoming a threat. I encouraged him to make eye contact, speak directly with people, flirt with women he was attracted to, and do all of the other things that would make him a threat. It was only through this form of bold action that he would realize that people respond positively to assertiveness.

This section highlights the ways you might be playing small and holding yourself back. This behavior might be manifesting itself in your body language, tone of voice, or in what you choose to say (or not to say). Becoming aware of these patterns of inhibition can help you choose an alternative that allows you to let more of yourself out when you are around others.

Turn Down The Filter

When we have spent years making sure people will like us, and will therefore not reject us, it is easy to develop a habit of accommodation and self-censorship. People with social anxiety are often highly sensitive and perceptive, with an uncanny ability to determine what someone is feeling and what they might need to hear. You also might have a strong ability to determine what the conversational *hot buttons* are, and know how to avoid them. You are careful to never offend, never step on another's toes, never interrupt, and never be rude or abrupt.

In order to pull this off, we must develop a filter or screen that blocks out anything that might be offensive or lead to disapproval. Everything we might say or do passes through this filter, which blocks anything that seems risky, offensive, inappropriate, forward, or otherwise disagreeable. While this might serve to minimize disagreement and increase the approval you receive, it also requires a lot of work in the background. It greatly reduces your ability to be spontaneous, relaxed, and free flowing in your speech and actions. It is like you are always on guard, making sure that you say and do the *right* things.

A major step in being bolder in the world, and putting yourself out there more, is to turn your filter down. This means expressing more of what you really think, feel, and want for others around you to see.

ShyQuote:
When he was telling me about his job, I had no idea what he did exactly. In fact, I don't know the first thing about his field. I didn't want to offend him or look stupid, so I smiled and nodded and tried to follow along.

Turning your filter down involves paying attention to what you are curious about during conversations, what you want, and what your perspective or opinion is, then sharing these things more freely. In short, it means blurting out more questions, thoughts, and curiosities. When someone shares a story and you are curious about a detail, it means interjecting, asking him to clarify the thing you're curious about. If someone shares a detail you don't understand or can't follow, ask if she'll explain it more.

We fear that if we ask questions, people will think we are stupid or nosy. The truth is that others may have the same question as us—we just happen to be the only ones bold enough to ask. In addition, the more you accept *all* of yourself, the easier it will be for you to admit you do not know something, and therefore need additional clarification. As far as being too nosy or inappropriate with our questions, it can be helpful to realize that many people find all sorts of conversations boring. In fact, we are all tired of talking about the same things, from the overly polite pleasantries about the weather, to what happened in the big game.

When someone asks others intriguing questions about themselves, their lives, and their interests, it sparks an enjoyable, memorable conversation. The majority of the time, instead of coming across as nosy, others will see your curiosity as endearing and genuine.

Turning down your filter also involves blurting out more of your perceptions, ideas, reactions, and opinions. This can be an uncomfortable prospect if you have spent years keeping those things to yourself, for fear that people will consider you pushy, opinionated, self-centered, or ignorant. While there are undoubtedly some people who come across in these ways, the vast majority of shy people do not have to worry about this. You have spent much of your life holding back your thoughts and opinions, and your filter is turned up incredibly high. Even if you turned it down by 80%, you would still probably be more considerate, tactful, and respectful of other's opinions than a majority of people.

When someone is sharing and it reminds you of something you read, saw or thought about recently, try mentioning it. Throw your two cents into the conversation.

What to expect

As you practice turning down your filter, you will most likely encounter an obstacle, followed by a greater sense of liberation. Initially, when you blurt out a question or say something that comes to mind during a conversation, you might feel even *more* uncomfortable than when you were struggling to find things to say. After the conversation, you might relive the moment again and again, feeling more embarrassed or humiliated each time. You might even resolve internally that you will never blurt anything out again.

Remember the backlash discussion earlier in this chapter? Do not worry, this might simply be a sign that you are taking a step forward and using your voice more. Your inner critic hates when you blurt things out without filtering them, because it fears you might say something people will judge or criticize.

The key here, just as with any other backlash, is to use your skills of self-acceptance and self-compassion to weather the backlash storm. You can try compassionate letter writing, dialoguing with your critic (see Chapter 7), or talking with a close friend our counselor. Stay as patient and compassionate with yourself as you can during the barrage of internal criticism. Doing so will allow you to continue on your journey of speaking up more and putting your authentic self out into the world.

Whatever you do, be skeptical of your critic's claims that turning down the filter is bad, and that you should never do something like that again. This is simply more propaganda to keep you under internal tyrannical control. Instead, dig deep to find the courage to be who you really are around others, which includes sharing your spontaneous feelings, reactions, perceptions and opinions. This is you sharing the gift of yourself, which is essential to feeling connected to those around you.

TURN THE VOLUME UP

Another way we silence ourselves, aside from censoring what we say, is to literally speak more quietly. This is an incredibly common pattern in shyness and social anxiety, and it conveys quite a bit about what we think of ourselves. The general attitude of social anxiety is one of discounting ourselves. In essence it is the belief that we do not matter, that we are not very valuable, and by extension what we think, feel, and say does not really matter or add value to those around us.

When you believe this, you will keep most of what you think and feel to yourself. After all, who would really care anyway? As a result, if we are in a situation where we are forced to speak, we do the best we can to discount what we are saying. We speak in a quiet, hesitant manner. We may mumble or trail off at the end of a statement. This makes us difficult to hear and understand, and easy to write-off as unconvincing and insignificant.

This is one of the many self-fulfilling prophecies of shyness. We assume others do not care what we have to say, so we communicate in a way that makes others less interested in what we have to say. In order to free your voice, speak up for yourself, and take bold action towards being yourself in the world. Consciously speaking louder can produce a powerful shift in how you feel and in how others respond to you.

The most basic way to begin this practice is to consciously increase your speaking volume to a level that is in the normal-to-loud range. This is the volume that is loud enough so that everyone can hear what you are saying, but it is not so loud that it seems unusual. In addition, you can practice counteracting the tendency to trail off or mumble at the end of a phrase by consciously increasing your volume as you speak a phrase. When you do this, the last word you say will be slightly louder than the first one you spoke. This experiment can help you learn and practice one of the most important secrets of communication.

It is not what you say... it's how you say it
When you are communicating, whether it is with one person in a quiet coffee shop, or with three hundred people during a

presentation, *how* you are speaking has a greater impact than what you actually say. The vast majority of your communication comes from your body language and the tone of your voice. In order to communicate in a way that is more empowered, clear, confident and direct, the most important thing to do is to speak in a manner that showcases these qualities. This includes speaking slightly louder, possessing a sense of certainty in what you are saying, and ending your sentences with force and conviction.

At the top of my personal fear hierarchy for many years was public speaking. This is a very common fear, and you might have this at the top of your hierarchy as well. I hated it. I was terrified for days before, could barely breathe during the presentation, and then ruminated about it for days afterwards. Speaking in front of a group was one of the worst experiences I could imagine. As I worked through the same process that you are working through now, I began to move towards what scares me, rather than away from it. I started seeking out places to practice speaking, including a local Toastmasters chapter. I continued down this path for many years, regularly moving towards what scared me most.

At this point, I am comfortable speaking with a large group of people, and my anxiety ranges from mild to moderate for about one day leading up to the presentation. Once the presentation starts, I generally have a very good time and feel exhilarated by the opportunity to communicate a message to so many people at once.

During my public speaker training, I learned it is inevitable that I will sometimes misspeak, stumble over my words, or make some sort of mistake. This prospect used to terrify me, and it was one of the reasons I avoided speaking so avidly. But what I realized was that it did not seem to matter when I made a mistake, if I applied the principle described in this section. I discovered I could mispronounce a word and even say something that did not quite make sense as long as I finished the statement with a tone of conviction, authority, and confidence.

The first time I stumbled across this principle, I thought it was a fluke. But as I practiced doing this each time I made a mistake, it became very clear to me that people did not seem to notice the misstep, as long as I concluded my sentence in a confident manner. This translates to any conversation you have with any number of people. Even if you do not plan on speaking publicly, this communication secret can help ensure that others are hearing you clearly, and are listening to what you're saying. It will also help you gain greater respect in your relationships with friends, coworkers, and life partners.

In order to get comfortable with the volume of your voice and speaking with conviction, I highly recommend you find a private place to practice, whether in your car during your commute, in the shower, or sitting in your kitchen. Wherever you choose, make sure you are comfortable, and experiment with projecting your voice, concluding sentences with force, and finishing your statements with conviction. The more you practice, the more it will naturally emerge in conversations with others.

EYES ON THE HORIZON

One of the most powerful—and often overlooked—forms of communication we use every day has nothing to do with the words we use. It is what we communicate with our eyes. The way we look at someone can communicate trust, distrust, dislike, hatred, admiration, joy, and even love.

When we want to connect with someone on a deeper level, we almost always choose a face-to-face interaction. This way, we can look into the other person's eyes as we talk. When falling in love, we can spend hours simply gazing into the eyes of our beloved.

One of the most inhibiting effects of social anxiety is that it dramatically limits the amount of eye contact you might be willing to engage in. It can be hard to make eye contact with new people and strangers, and it can be difficult to sustain it during a conversation. When anxious, you might tend to look away frequently, and keep your eyes cast down towards the floor.

ShyQuote:
I feel like if I look at people in the eye for too long it's going to freak them out. They might think I am hitting on them, or threatening them or something.

Because of these fears, the most common response from people with social anxiety is to avoid eye contact as much as possible. If we do make eye contact, we can have an immediate, knee-jerk reaction to look away from the other person. The idea of sustaining eye contact can feel incredibly uncomfortable, and can produce a great deal of anxiety. Our natural inclination is to avoid it. By now, however, you have realized that the pattern of avoidance produces relief in the short term, but tends to cause more fear and restriction down the road.

One simple way to shift your pattern of eye contact is to consciously walk with your head held up high and your eyes on the level of the horizon. It is so common for us to walk and move with our eyes cast slightly downward, lost in our own world of thoughts. Instead, you can practice walking with your eyes directly ahead, taking in the world around you. After all, putting yourself out into the world involves looking at the world—directly in the eye.

A powerful way to overcome your fear of eye contact is to engage in the *Smile and Hello Practice* discussed earlier. This involves walking down a busy street and making eye contact with as many people as you can. You can get their attention by smiling and loudly saying "hello!" or "hi there!"

You can also choose to increase eye contact with strangers throughout the day. You can experiment by looking at people's eyes as you walk down the street. If they return your gaze, you can simply smile and continue to look into their eyes as you walk past. In response to the thought of doing this experiment, your mind might be saying:

Wait a minute—people will think I'm a freak. They will feel violated or irritated by me looking at them.

It is very common to feel frightened or hesitant about doing this experiment beforehand, especially if you have spent years avoiding eye contact. In doing this experiment hundreds of times, both on my own and with clients, I have found that nothing bad ever really happens. In fact, this kind of eye contact tends to bring people out of their shells, and I end up having more spontaneous conversations with strangers.

A final way to experiment with exposure to eye contact is to decide to sustain eye contact with people when you are listening to them. As they are talking, allow yourself to look directly into one of their eyes. As you do this, you can focus some of your awareness on the sensations in your feet on the floor, and the air coming in and out of your lungs as you breathe. This will help you remain present while you practice making sustained eye contact.

The benefits of becoming more comfortable with eye contact greatly outweigh the discomfort of the process. Eye contact is one of the most powerfully connecting forces between humans, and the more comfortable you become with it, the more you will be able to feel a deep sense of connection with the people in your life.

Nine

THE COURAGE TO BE VULNERABLE

Social anxiety comes from the fear that we are not enough and are therefore not lovable. This fear makes the idea of being *found out, judged,* and *rejected* terrifying, and we avoid certain aspects of life at all costs. This leads to a life of playing small, avoiding connection, and steering clear of anything that might cause judgment or rejection. The more we avoid, the smaller our life becomes, and the more limited our future looks.

The solution offered in this book is one of knowing and respecting yourself, accepting and loving yourself as you are, and taking bold action in the world around you. Through these actions you learn that your fears are merely shadows that pose no significant threats. You learn that most of the time people do *not* reject you, and that even when they do you are able to handle the discomfort that follows.

The final, and deepest form of exposure is to actually learn how to reveal your authentic self to the world around you. This involves revealing yourself *as you actually are,* not as you think you are supposed to be in order to be loved.

Each one of us has an outer layer of our personality. This is called a *persona* or mask and it is what we use to go about our day-to-day life. When someone asks us how we are doing, we immediately respond with "fine," or "not bad." This is the mask, and we use it throughout the day in dozens of interactions. We rarely reveal what is behind the mask, whether it is our true thoughts about someone, our beliefs, or our feelings in the moment.

The mask is an essential part of life that helps us function in our world. Is there a problem with the mask? Yes. When we believe we have to wear the mask at all times because of our fear of judgment, then we are unable to reveal our true selves.

This leads to the circular fear of social anxiety:

I am afraid people will judge me, but if they knew I was afraid of being judged, they would judge me even more.

This fear blocks us from revealing ourselves *as we are* in the moment, and keeps the mask frozen in place.

CERTAINLY THEY CANNOT SEE THIS

In order to fully connect with others and be at ease in yourself, you must engage in the following process:

Look inside to see what you are really thinking and feeling, then reveal that with people with whom you feel safe and who are not likely to harshly reject you. Repeat.

Each time you struggle with a feeling or experience, instead of hiding it and using it as evidence that you are flawed, what if you were able to share it with the people in your life? This thought is often appalling at first to people with social anxiety. Certainly, *I could not share that with **anyone**.* Really? No one? The most powerful cure for shame is to uncover it and share it with others who will understand and identify with your struggle. When you are feeling anxious about talking with someone, have you ever considered simply stating that?

At first this seems like the complete opposite of what you *should* be doing. Common wisdom says that if you are attracted to someone and are having a conversation with them, you cannot tell them you are nervous because they will think you are weak and pathetic. But have you actually tried it?

Adam, a client of mine, regularly struggled in the area of dating and relationships. He hated how nervous he became when he was talking with a woman he found attractive. He would do whatever he could to hide this shameful secret, and learned how to appear more confident from the outside. In addition, he used his sharp wit to hide any feelings of anxiety by keeping the women he talked with on their toes.

While he had learned to hide his feelings successfully, he discovered this did not make him more successful in his love life. On the contrary, he found he had a harder time connecting with women he really liked. He had several experiences in a row in which he went on one date with a woman and she failed to return his calls for a second date.

As we discussed the topic of vulnerability, I asked him if he had ever directly told one of the women he was dating that he was nervous. Initially, he dismissed this suggestion as completely ludicrous and unhelpful. However, several months—and several failed dates—later he was more curious about "trying this vulnerable thing," as he put it.

One session he kept repeating the phrase, "When she sees this about me, she will *certainly* reject me. Saying I am nervous is like admitting I am a weakling who cannot handle being with her. She will lose all respect for me." I agreed that this could possibly happen, and suggested he view it as an experiment like one of the items from his fear hierarchy. Perhaps he would experience a different outcome than the one he was afraid of. Unconvinced, but desperate, he decided to give it a try.

"There is one caveat," I said just before our session was over. He looked at me expectantly. "Being vulnerable means actually sharing what you are feeling—not making a sarcastic joke about it, or saying how pathetic she must think you are. It involves saying something really simply and honestly such as, 'I was really nervous before you came to pick me up. Ha, I spent thirty minutes figuring out where we could eat. I guess on some level I am hoping you will approve of me.'"

He stared at me with wide eyes, slowly shaking his head from left to right. His mouth had started to hang open slightly as he heard the vulnerable phrases I offered him. He pulled himself together and said he would give it a shot, in a tone that did not sound particularly convincing to either of us.

Much to my surprise, when he returned to the next session, he was beaming a bright smile as he entered my office. He told me he ran into one of the women who didn't return his calls and he decided to "try the vulnerable thing."

"She said she couldn't tell if I liked her when we were on the date, that I seemed disinterested, which made her nervous. She actually really liked me but assumed it wasn't mutual!"

This was a major turning point for Adam. He had taken the leap and dared to be vulnerable only to discover that his worst fears proved false. Instead of being met with harsh rejection and ridicule, he was met with kindness and shared vulnerability. Best of all, he felt a sense of excitement and connection with this woman, which is something he had not felt in all his years of living behind his mask.

A Life of Courage

At this point, you have a choice about the kind of life you would like to live. While we always have this choice, some moments make that clearer than others.

- You have read about the cause of your social anxiety—an old belief that you are somehow just not good enough and unworthy of love.
- You learned all the ways this belief remains in place, including your harsh inner critic.

- You have also learned how to liberate yourself from this restricting idea.
- You learned how to identify who you really are, what you really want, and what you have to offer the world around you.
- You learned how to treat yourself with kindness, compassion, warmth and respect.
- You learned how to take new actions in the world that will help you dispel the old belief that no one could ever love you as you are.

After reading this book, a new door is now open for you. You have the option to step through it, into a life of courage that involves challenging old ideas, trying new things, and revealing your authentic self to the people around you. This life demands that you move towards what scares you, step off the bleachers and onto the field, and face the inevitable failures and rejections along your path towards success. Most importantly, this life demands a relentless courage to be on your own side no matter what happens. To choose again and again to love and accept yourself as you are, and to be willing to try again. To put yourself out there again, ask for a date again, love again, and to offer who you are to the world again.

This door will not remain open forever. After you have put this book down, it can be easy to forget the encouragement to be kinder to yourself or to try something new. The old propaganda campaign will slowly influence you over time to believe that things cannot change and you are stuck the way you are.

This door is open only for a short while, and you must make the decision to leap through it to the unknown that waits on the other side. I encourage you with all of my heart to make the jump. While the potential fall might be scary, the world around you will hold you up. There are thousands of people out there who want to be your friend, and thousands more who want to date you, sleep with you, marry you, and start a family with you. The world is waiting for you to show up as your full, authentic self. Do not keep it waiting.

May you have the courage to be who you are.

Recommended Resources

Self-Esteem and Cognitive Therapy

Intimate Connections (New York: Penguin Group, 1985)
David Burns

Self-Esteem (Oakland: New Harbinger, 2000)
Matthew McKay and Patrick Fanning

Feeling Good (New York: HarperCollins, 1980)
David Burns

Changing Behavior

Feel The Fear And Do It Anyway (New York: Random House, 1987)
Susan Jeffers

It's Not Over Until I Win (New York: Fireside, 1997)
Les Brown

Conduct a YouTube search for the following Les Brown lectures:
"You Deserve…!"
"It's Possible"

Healthy Selfishness (Des Moines: Meredith Books, 2006)
Richard Heller and Rachael Heller

MINDFULNESS AND SELF-ACCEPTANCE

Radical Acceptance (New York: Bantam Dell, 2004)
Tara Brach

Full Catastrophe Living (New York: Bantam Dell, 1990)
Jon Kabat-Zinn

Self-Compassion (New York: HarperCollins, 2012)
Kristin Neff

The Mindful Path to Self-Compassion (New York: Guilford 2009)
Christopher Germer, PhD

I Thought It Was Just Me (New York: Penguin Group, 2007)
Brene Brown

MEN'S PSYCHOLOGY

The Way Of The Superior Man (Boulder: Sounds True 1997)
David Deida

No More Mr. Nice Guy (Philadelphia: Barnes & Noble Publishing, 2003)
Robert Glover

Double Your Dating (E-Book product, available at
www.doubleyourdating.com)
David DeAngelo

SOCIAL CONFIDENCE PROGRAMS

Confidence Unleashed (www.ConfidenceUnleashedNow.com)
Dr. Aziz Gazipura

30 Days To Dating Mastery (www.30DaysToDatingMastery.com)
Dr. Aziz Gazipura

Dr. Aziz is a clinical psychologist and one of the world's leading experts on social confidence. After struggling with social anxiety himself for over ten years, he eventually sought help. As he started to see a positive shift in his life, he became obsessed with how he could overcome the social fears that held him back.

He read hundreds of books on psychology and personal development, listened to thousands of hours of audio programs, and attended dozens of seminars and intensive immersion workshops. He sought out the help of coaches and "dating

gurus" he located on the internet, and was willing to try anything to see if it produced a positive result.

He began to study clinical psychology at Palo Alto and Stanford
Universities in order to more deeply understand how people can
transform their attitudes, perceptions, and their lives. There he
sought out individualized training with Dr. Matthew May and
Dr. David Burns – leading figures in the field of Cognitive Behavioral Therapy.

In 2011, Dr. Aziz started The Center For Social Confidence,
which is dedicated to helping men break through their shyness
and social anxiety. Through his unique blend of compassion,
humor, and personal courage, Dr. Aziz has helped thousands
of men all over the world increase their confidence. Through
confidence coaching, audio and video programs, podcasts, a
detailed blog, and intensive weekend workshops, Dr. Aziz lives
out his mission: To help every man who is stuck in shyness
liberate himself to pursue the woman, career, and life he has
always dreamed of.

He lives in Portland, Oregon with his wife Candace and
soon-to-be-born son (who he claims will be the "most socially
confident badass kid in the world.")

65461586R00139

Made in the USA
Charleston, SC
28 December 2016